Erik
Estrada

Erik Estrada

My Road from

Harlem to Hollywood

with Davin Seay

William Morrow and Company, Inc.
New York

Library of Congress Cataloging-in-Publication Data
Estrada, Erik, 1949–
    Erik Estrada : my road from Harlem to Hollywood / Erik Estrada
with Davin Seay.
      p. cm.
    Includes index.
    ISBN 0-688-14293-1
    1. Estrada, Erik, 1949- . 2. Actors—United States—
Biography.
I. Seay, Davin. II. Title.
PN2287.E76A3   1997
791.45'028'092—dc20
  [B]   96-43864
                                        CIP

Printed in the United States of America
FIRST EDITION

1 2 3 4 5 6 7 8 9 10

BOOK DESIGN BY LAURA HOUGH

To children of every ethnic background:

Be proud of your history—it's the key to your future

Davin Seay would like to dedicate his work to

Miriam Kolisch, with love, admiration, and gratitude

Special thanks to Konrad Leh—

your energy, insight, and creativity

have re-invented my career.

Tu Amigo Siempre

Erik

Introduction

"What you see is what you get."

It's an all-purpose expression you hear a lot these days, from opening the door on a blind date to closing a deal on a used car. Everyone knows what it means: no bells and whistles, no smoke and mirrors, no dog-and-pony show. It's about honesty and integrity, about walking the walk and talking the talk . . . in short, it's about being real.

But sometimes what you see isn't what you get. Sometimes perception is the only reality, fantasy becomes fact, and lies turn into the story of your life. Sometimes what you see, and what you get, are only what someone else wants you to see . . . and buy . . . and believe.

I know. From firsthand experience, I know what it's like to be built into something I never dreamed I could be and, just as quickly, torn down to something I never want to be again. I know what it's like to have money and power and prestige working for you . . . and against you. And I know what it's like to step outside that illusion, to stake your claim and pay the price. I've been there and done that and lived to tell the tale.

But for me, there's another side to getting what you see and seeing what you get. It's about looking at my own reflection in the mirror every morning; about knowing that, through good times and bad, monster success and miserable failure, I've tried to stay true to myself—to who I am and what I believe. It's about admitting my faults, weaknesses, and mistakes as much as acknowledging my accomplishments and achievements. It's about being able to stare at that familiar reflection without shame or guilt, and if I can do that, I know I can look anyone in the eye and truthfully say, "What you see is what you get."

Some people find that hard to believe. It's an actor's job, after all, to pretend, to wear masks and play a role. And at the end of the day, when the lights go down and the curtain closes, we're supposed to step out of character and back to being who we really are, private people hidden from the public's prying eyes.

But it has never really worked quite that way for me. Whether it's in the movies or on TV, up onstage or up close and personal, there's a big part of me in most of the roles I've portrayed. Sure, I can play against type as well as anyone, take on personalities and project emotions that I don't own. That's what acting is all about. But throughout my career what has counted the most is the connection between my audience and me . . . the real me, behind the part and beyond the celebrity status. It's a bond that has linked me with people I've never even met, people who believed in me, even when I didn't believe in myself. That's an honor and a privilege I don't think I'll ever be able to repay.

But I'm going to try. That's one of the reasons for this book. The best way I know to thank the people around the world who have had faith in me, hoping for the best even through the worst, is to tell the truth, the whole truth and nothing but. I want to set the record straight, to dispel the lies and state the facts, once and for all.

And while I know there might be a lot of satisfaction to be gained from telling my side of the story for the first time, there's something more important here than putting a fresh coat of polish on my reputation. And that's letting all of you know that while maybe I wasn't always the hero you wanted me to be, I was never the villain you were told about either. The simple fact is, I'm just like anybody else: a man who's made some mistakes, learned some lessons, and gotten a second chance. With Erik Estrada, what you see really is what you get.

So who does that face in the mirror belong to? Who is Erik Estrada? Well, a lot of people, even today, still think I'm a veteran of the California Highway Patrol, while a lot of TV fans South of the Border firmly believe I'm mixed up in a torrid love affair. The truth is, I really don't mind being associated with the role of Officer Poncherello, my character in *CHiPs*, or Johnny, the part I played in the Latin telenovella *Dos Mujeres, Un Camino*. Whatever their faults and flaws, or however one-dimensional they might have sometimes seemed, I found a part of myself, or a quirk or character trait I could relate to, in those fictional heroes. I feel the same about many of my portrayals, from the streetwise punk in *The Cross and the Switchblade* to the rookie cop in *The New Centurions* to the champion boxer in the TV movie *Honey Boy*.

At the same time, of course, I've played parts that I'm not exactly proud of, when all that mattered was looking good, reading my lines, and living up to the stereotype. Then again, what actor hasn't had his share of jobs without passion?

But there's one role that I never auditioned for, a character I've played that had nothing to do with me. Sure, he had my face and my name, but for all the things he did, and for all the things people said about him, he might just as well have come from another planet.

I used to see that Erik Estrada on the cover of tabloid newspapers at the supermarket checkout. I read articles about him in *TV Guide*

under headlines like THE TIME BOMB IS STILL TICKING. I heard whispered rumors about the tantrums he'd throw and the outrageous
demands he'd make; about his arrogance and ego, his sexual appetite
and violent outbursts; about drug abuse and black magic rituals and
other outrageous accusations and innuendos that clung to him like
a bad odor.

And I wondered, "Who is this guy? Who are they talking about?"
Sure, that was my photo up there on all those lurid covers, but the
stories they told weren't about me. I never did those things, or even
dreamed of doing them.

But what can you do when everyone believes the worst about
you? Where do you turn to let the truth be known, to clear your
name and save your reputation?

For a long time, the only place I could find was inside my own
head, nursing my wounds far from the screaming headlines and the
merciless drumbeat of scandal. Despite all the tough-guy roles I'd
played in my career, all the macho charisma I'd learned to cultivate,
the bottom line was that the lies hurt and that pain drove me inward, away from the glaring spotlights and relentless gossip.

I came up from the streets of Spanish Harlem, where you learn right
away to protect yourself, to hide your vulnerabilities and never let
your opponent see you flinch. And for a lot of years, that's the way
I tried to deal with the storm that swirled around me, leading with
my jaw, giving back as good as I got, and taking my punishment
like a man.

But the truth is, you can live that way for only so long. It gets
lonely with only your anger and resentment to keep you company.
There comes a time when the only way to move on is to make
peace; the only way to get better is to stop being bitter. Sure, I've
been lied about, called a temperamental egomaniac, a wife beater,

and worse, and had my name dragged through the mud in the pages of everything from the *National Enquirer* to *TV Guide*. I've seen my career go up in smoke and my personal life fall to pieces. I've had enough trials and tribulations for a dozen soap operas, and plenty of reasons to blame the world and feel sorry for myself.

But I've had just as many reasons to feel bountifully blessed, fortunate and favored and just plain lucky. I've had a chance to live a life most people only dream about; to move in circles worlds away from my Harlem roots, to rub elbows with the rich and famous and make love to some very beautiful, talented, and accomplished women. I've had the opportunity to make my mark and be a star and hear my name called out by strangers when I walk down the street.

And it's been great, even when I knew, somewhere in the back of my brain, that it was only going to last as long as the Nielsens stayed high, the box office broke big, and I kept seeing my face on the magazine covers. Still, while it lasted, parts of that life were every bit as great as I could have imagined. Anyone who tells you a different story about fame . . . well, let's just say they're trying to keep a good thing to themselves.

In the pages of this book that quest for the best plays a big part, just as ambition, drive, and the need to prove myself are a big part of who I am, who I'll always be. And if the story of my life proves anything, it's that while you may be able to take a dream away from a man, you can never take a man away from his dream. Ever since I can remember, I've dreamed big and I've been lucky enough to see some of those dreams come true.

But when all's said and done, the story of Erik Estrada isn't about dreaming big and grabbing the brass ring. It's about finding peace in the simple things, about learning the lessons of life by living it one day at a time. It's about taking responsibility, about forgiving and forgetting, about finally discovering what's really important.

When you close the covers on my life story, my hope is that you'll share some of the sense of gratitude that I feel today, not for the dizzy heights I've attained but for the everyday miracles that we all share.

I've found someone to love and someone who loves me too. I'm proud of the work I do and the place I've made for myself. I honor my family and cherish my children, taking care of them as I take care of myself. I've let go of yesterday and look forward to tomorrow.

And sometimes, on a warm Southern California afternoon, when the sea breeze blows the shadow of clouds across the valley floor, I can sit on my front porch and smoke a good cigar and think back, with a laugh or a sigh, on how it all came down.

How could I ask for anything more?

Erik

Estrada

Chapter One

Any man's beginning reaches back past his point of origin—the time, date, and place when he made his grand entrance—to the deepest roots of his heritage. Who we are depends on where we came from, our people, our culture, and the way of life we carry with us from cradle to grave.

In my career, that question of heritage has always been more than a little blurred. My dark skin and Latin looks have landed me roles as everything from Italian to Chicano to the all-purpose Hispanic. And for a lot of Spanish-speaking people, I was something of a role model, one of their own who made it big.

Well, I wish I could say that I was aware of my heritage, proud of my people and ready to be an example for everyone who saw me as one of their own. But the truth is, for a long time I never really thought of myself in terms of my cultural credentials. I guess the best indication of that is the fact that, up until a few years ago, I never spoke anything more than pidgin Spanish. I never sought out spokesman status for causes that concerned Latinos. I never even thought of myself as breaking down race barriers in Hollywood. I was just happy to be working, whether I got the job for my talent or my skin tone.

That would all change in time, as I came to realize not only how much I owed to my Puerto Rican lineage, but how much I wanted to give back to my people. Strong family ties, fierce loyalties, and passionate emotions wouldn't be stereotypes of Puerto Ricans unless there was at least some truth in them, and I share many of those traits. But growing up, I never thought as much of what made me different from others as what I had in common with them: I was American-born, native of the greatest city in the world, and mixed up in the melting pot of a legendary neighborhood.

The neighborhood was uptown Manhattan, where I was born in Harlem Hospital, March 16, 1949. The name on the birth certificate was Henry Estrada, but it wasn't long before everyone was calling me by the affectionate nickname "Papo," which was the Puerto Rican equivalent of the Jewish "Tatilla" or the Italian "Bambino"—just another all-purpose handle for any cute kid.

Cute, and in my case, very cuddly. I was born at nine pounds ten ounces. Considering that my mom is a tiny woman, tipping the scale at no more than a hundred pounds soaking wet, it must have been a memorable occasion for her. Thankfully, she's the forgiving type.

And she had a lot to forgive in her early years. She had been raised in the Puerto Rican city of Mayagüez, where my grandfather, Don Pino Cardona, worked a prosperous sugarcane farm that stretched up the whole side of a lush green mountain outside of town.

The Cardona family was prosperous by island standards, with a family market that they operated along with the farm. But like simple people everywhere, they dreamed of a better life, one that included all the modern conveniences that they saw advertised in the pages of glossy American magazines. In that postwar period of optimism and opportunity, anything seemed possible, I guess, even selling off the farm, packing up a sprawling clan, and making the epic migration to *Norteamérica*.

By this time my mother was already married to a handsome Mayagüez farm boy named Rinaldo Estrada. He must have been quite a charmer in his day because my mother, even though she's one of the warmest, most nurturing people I've ever known, isn't one to be too easily swept off her feet. But whatever he was selling my Mom was buying, and it wasn't long before they were married and a daughter was born and given my mother's name, Carmen.

It's hard for me to imagine that time in my family's history, so full of hope and potential as they looked to a new life in a new land. My grandfather, as the patriarch of the clan, made the decision to immigrate. He picked New York City as the family's destination, based on the tales of fabled wealth that came back to the island. New York, letters home promised, was a place where a man could make his fortune by his wits, hard work, and maybe a little favor from the Virgin Mary or a patron saint. It was where you went when you wanted to start again, to break free of the destiny you were born to and fashion a new future for your children. You have to admire a breed of men who would risk everything for that chance, and there was no one I admired more than my grandfather.

It was Don Pino who filled the role of father in my early life, a role my real father had turned his back on almost from the moment I was born. Actually, as a child I never knew who my dad really was, and by the time I was old enough to figure out what had happened to him, it was already too late to heal the wounds.

If you've never really known someone, never had a chance to find out what you're missing by not having him around, how can you be resentful toward him? There are times when I realize that I've handled difficult situations in certain ways—by butting heads, digging in my heels, or throwing a punch—because I never had a dad to teach me a better way. It is times like those when I wish he'd been there for me, but with that wish comes sadness, not anger.

When the Cardona clan arrived in New York, they could easily have laid claim to a whole block of Spanish Harlem. There were my grandfather and grandmother, my dad and my mom, and my sister in Mom's arms. There were my uncles Frankie and Pete and

3

William and Edwin and my aunts Lucy and Haydee: Of the eleven sons and daughters, six made the trip while the rest stayed behind.

But instead of having a block, on a street paved with gold, they all ended up in a three-room railroad flat in the projects on the mean streets of 103rd Street and First Avenue.

I sometimes try to put myself in their place, setting down their battered cardboard suitcases in that cramped apartment, with all the noisy traffic surging by outside those grimy windows, in a country where no one knew their names or cared about their hopes and fears. Did they wonder how they ended up so far from the green mountains and simple traditions of their homeland? Did they count the cost of chasing their dreams and find the price too high? Did they try to hide their fear, uncertainty, and isolation from each other? Or did they just begin at the beginning, unpacking and cleaning and making a place for themselves in this strange new land?

My guess is, a little bit of all those feelings passed among them, settling down in different ways on each member of my family. For my grandfather, responsibility rested easily on his broad shoulders. For my aunts and uncles, the excitement of the new world was more than enough to dampen their doubts. For my mother, this was one more test in a lifetime of tests to come. But for my father, the freedom of America was more than he could handle.

Maybe it was the barrier of language. Maybe it was all the invisible obstacles that stood between a poor immigrant and that good life on display in the store windows around him. Maybe it was that sense of purpose and identification that would come from being part of a street gang. Or maybe it was just that Rinaldo Estrada never had what it took to make a life for himself and his family. It's not my place to judge my father. Of all the people who suffered from the tragedy of his life, he's the one who suffered most.

After the family's arrival, my father tried his best to help support the household, but the menial jobs that were available to a young immigrant weren't exactly what he had imagined the American

Dream to be all about. He and the rest of his brothers and sisters enjoyed a pretty good life back in Puerto Rico, and the shock of arriving someplace where no one knew who you were or even wanted to know, was very disillusioning. It wasn't too long before he began hanging out on street corners and in pool halls with all the other unemployed, restless young Puerto Ricans who felt as if their lives had reached a blind alley. From there it was only a short step to drugs, and after that, the all-too-familiar spiral of addiction, crime, and the death sentence of a heroin habit. There's nothing so special about my father's sad fate. It's happening every day, all around us in ghetto flats and back alleys from coast to coast. And in his case, as in all those other cases, the only thing that matters is how the people who are being sucked into that fate find a way to survive and a reason to keep going.

And that's exactly what my mother did. Some people might consider it a cold move to toss a junkie out on the street like so much trash, but my mother really didn't have much choice. With an infant son and a two-year-old daughter, as part of an extended family hanging on by a financial thread, where anyone who wasn't pulling his or her own weight was pulling down the rest, it was a simple matter of survival. And once the size of the monkey on my father's back became clear, she never looked back. She threw him out, once and forever, to live a desperate, hand-to-mouth existence on the hard streets of New York City, hustling for enough money to feed his habit.

When he left, my father took all my mother's hopes for a "happily ever after" with him. But if this was what life in America was all about, so be it. It was going to take more than drugs and poverty and a broken family to drag her down.

Because I was only three years old when my father left, I can count my memories of him on one hand. Some of them are good, like the time he gave me a silver dollar as a keepsake. It was the biggest, shiniest coin I'd ever seen and the only thing I ever remember getting from him. Maybe it seems strange that I can't recall more of someone who should have been one of the most important influences in my life. But that's just the point: To me, my father was nothing more than a ghost, leaving a ghostly trail through my early memories.

But I do have other memories, dim recollections from the back of my mind that I'd just as soon forget. Like the time I accidentally opened the bathroom door and saw him sitting on the toilet doing something I couldn't understand. He had his belt wrapped around his arm and a spoon was sitting on the counter. I can still smell the sharp scent of a burned match in that confined space and still see the look of anger mixed with shame in his eyes.

It wasn't until years later, as a teenager, when I happened to be watching an episode of Lee Marvin's M *Squad* on TV, that I finally put two and two together. The show was about drug dealers and the connection between the scene of a junkie shooting up and my father in the bathroom hit me between the eyes like a two-by-four.

Other memories would follow, mental snapshots of visiting my father in a hospital down on Delancey Street. He was laid out on clean bleached sheets, with both legs in big white plaster casts. I would find out only later that he'd been thrown from a third-story window by some pushers he'd stiffed, but at the time all I knew was that this skinny, hollow-eyed man with black curly hair was supposed to be my father. Later, when he was out of the hospital and living with his parents, I would be brought down to visit him. I remember pushing him through the crowded Delancey Street markets in his wheelchair and all the time feeling nothing, no sorrow, no pity, no rage, no regrets. He was a stranger.

When my dad left, so did my Uncle Pete, who had also picked up a taste for heroin and had taken to stealing from my grandmother to feed his habit. It was my grandfather who slammed the door on Pete, his own son, and for all the same reasons my mother had given her husband his walking papers. I like to think of it as strength of character, a hard-edged determination to do what had to be done, that my grandfather had passed down to my mother and that she, in turn, did her best to instill in me.

My mother and my grandfather were the center of my small world. From before I could remember, I had been without a real father, but they were determined to make up for his absence in every way they could. Because of them, because of their love, it would be a long time before I realized what I was missing. But, of course, eventually I would come to find out what living without a father's guidance and support really meant. It was only when I realized how big a hole he'd left behind that I fully understood how much they both had tried to make up for the void.

As hard and unforgiving as it may seem for her to have turned her back on her husband, my mother instinctively knew that the drug demon he was dealing with was stronger then either one of them. And she was right. My dad continued to scrape by in the shadowland of the junkie, living on the streets and supporting his habit through petty crime. But he would never be able to find his way back into the real world again. She did the only thing she could, despite the pity and compassion she must have felt for him.

Because that's the kind of person she was, warm and giving and big-hearted to a fault. Another of the life lessons she tried to teach me early on was that we're put on this earth to try to help one another. And that wasn't just some pie-in-the-sky sentiment for her. She found ways to make that lesson real.

My mother was always taking in strays, which is why, even to this day, my own house is filled with cats and dogs I've pulled in off the streets. And for her, the impulse to help, to offer shelter and a warm meal to those in need, went further than junkyard dogs and alley cats. That's where Joey comes in. I'll never forget the day she walked into the apartment leading a teenage kid with slicked-back hair and a cigarette hanging out of his mouth, and announced to all of us that we had a houseguest. Never mind where he was going to sleep or what he was going to eat, she'd made up her mind to take this particular hard case under her wing and that was that.

And Joey was about as hard a case as you could imagine. I was still just a kid, but even I recognized that this was one guy you didn't want to tangle with. He had a real attitude, cultivated on the corner of Ninetieth Street and Amsterdam Avenue, home turf for the Latin Counts. He was a warlord for the gang and a born troublemaker. His own parents must have thought him dangerous because they'd kicked him out on the street with nothing but the shirt on his back.

That's where my mother found him. What made her decide she could turn this walking felony around I'll never know, but she did. Joey, in time, became one of the family. To me, he was a big brother and one of the best and most loyal friends I've ever had.

Even back then, my mother wanted to make sure I knew who I was and where I'd come from. Maybe she was afraid that I'd fall into the same snare that had caught my dad, and that only a sense of pride and purpose would sustain me. But whatever the case, she wanted me to be proud of myself and my people, which is why one summer she told me I'd be going back to Puerto Rico with my aunt Haydee to visit with the relatives that had stayed behind.

It was a time I'll never forget; my first trip out of the projects and it might as well have been a trip to Venus, it was that strange and new. Puerto Rico was a paradise, green and growing and lush beyond any corner of Central Park I'd ever seen. I spent my days roaming through the jungle underbrush, swinging from the trees like a spider monkey, picking plantains right off the vine, or shaking an avocado tree until the ripe fruit fell all around me and I grabbed the biggest one to take home to my Aunt Hilda. She'd cut it up and mix it into a bowl of rice for the most delicious lunch I'd ever tasted.

When I wasn't Tarzan in the trees, I'd be out in the sugarcane fields, hacking down a thick stalk, then peeling it and sucking out the sweet juice, just like my cousins had taught me. Then, when I'd gotten out the last drop of that nectar, I'd throw the husk into the hog pen and laugh as the fat, pink pigs fought with each other over the sticky morsel. No wonder I threw a fit when it was time to leave, clinging to a palm tree as they tried to heave me into the car for the trip to the airport and back home.

But, of course, back home was where I ended up—sleeping in my little corner of the bedroom with Joey or, sometimes, after a bad dream, climbing into bed with my grandfather. As much as I loved and depended on my mother, it was my grandfather whom I sought to fill the void left by my father. To me, Don Pino was the measure of every good thing in my life, a pillar of quiet strength, full of the simple wisdom he had brought with him from the island.

Some of that wisdom and his old folkways didn't fit in too well in the modern world. Back in Puerto Rico, for instance, the only plumbing they had was outhouses, and the way you answered the call of nature was to squat on your haunches on the edge of the hole. Well, that was a tradition he carried with him to America, and when it came time for me to be toilet trained, he taught me to climb up on the bowl like a cat.

It seemed perfectly natural to me until, one day, the bathroom door flew open and there were three of my uncles, pointing and laughing at me as I squatted over the toilet like a peasant. I was mortified, unable to reach over to close the door, until my grandfather came along and chased them away with a string of vintage Puerto Rican curses.

Most of my earliest and best memories have something to do with Papa Don Pino. I can still hear my voice bouncing off the walls of the project buildings as I shouted up to him in his berth in the fourth-floor window of our apartment for a "nickie" to buy ice cream. The language we shared was a street mix of English and Spanish, the kind of slang that would make any proper linguist cringe. Instead of either "nickel" or "cinco centavos," it was "nickie." But somehow, even with all that weird Spanglish, we understood each other perfectly.

And it didn't take words—Spanish, English, or otherwise—for me to know that I was my grandfather's favorite. When he'd cook oatmeal for the family breakfast, mine was always the one mixed with real milk, while everyone else got the powdered stuff. One of my favorite treats was fruit juice, sugar, and Carnation evaporated milk that he'd mix and freeze in an ice tray, then pop out in cold little squares. With that deep rumbling laugh of his, he seemed to get as much pleasure watching me slurp them down one after the other as I did tasting that delicious creamy coolness on a hot summer day.

It was on one of those same blistering afternoons, with the sun glaring off the soft asphalt and radiating heat like a blast furnace, that my grandfather taught me one of the most important and enduring lessons of my young life.

At that time he had a job selling flavored ice out of a pushcart along Lenox Avenue. I always admired the way he filled an order, scraping shavings off the big ice block with a few deft strokes, forming it into a mound in the little paper cup and pouring out the bright-colored syrup with a grand flourish before handing it over with a broad smile. And I always felt so proud when the customer held out his nickel and Papa Don Pino would point to me, his honorary cashier. I'd take the shiny coin and drop it into the pocket of his big baggy pants and, for that moment, we were partners, businessmen plying our trade like real professionals.

One day, when we were heading home after a long and profitable run down Lenox Avenue, as we threaded through the shadows of the high buildings in the fading afternoon light, we came across a little girl, probably no more than four years old, sitting on the front stoop of one of the project buildings. She was crying, her dirty face was streaked with tears, and she was sucking her thumb and looking for all the world like the loneliest little kid in New York City.

My grandfather stopped right in front of her, reached into his pocket and pulled out a handful of nickels from the day's take. He reached over and, pulling that little girl's thumb out of her mouth, put the pile of coins in her palm. "Here," he said softly. "Go get something to eat."

I was only about five years old at the time, but I remember it like it was yesterday. I just couldn't understand how, after that long hot day selling ices, he could just hand over his hard-earned money without a second thought. I looked at him and he just smiled, the wrinkled skin crinkling at the corners of his eyes. "Come on," he said. "We're gonna be late for supper." And he left it at that.

It wouldn't be until years later that I really understood the lesson he taught me that day: Giving is something you do with your whole heart.

I've been trying to live up to that example ever since.

Chapter Two

Any authentic rags-to-riches story has to begin, of course, with the rags, which puts my story in a different category right from the start. The fact that my family was poor is pretty obvious. When you've got eight people living in a three-bedroom tenement, with everyone working night and day for minimum wage just to make ends meet, you're not exactly describing *Lifestyles of the Rich and Famous.*

But being poor is also an attitude, a frame of mind I just never remember being acquainted with. The fact is, I considered myself a lucky kid growing up. I never had to hang my head because someone was better than me, never felt the sting of shame over what I didn't have or the envy of wanting something someone else had. A lot of that, naturally, had to do with the fact that everyone else in the neighborhood was pretty much in the same place we were, scrimping and saving and living from week to week.

It's also true that I didn't know how the world was divided along racial lines. As much of a melting pot as New York City has always been, if you lived in my section of Spanish Harlem you were part of a close-knit community of Puerto Ricans who had claimed that little corner of the city as their own. We might have considered ourselves American first, but being from Puerto Rico, and being proud of the fact, ran a close second in the way we defined ourselves. We didn't let our poverty, or the color of our skin, tell us who we were or who we could become. Like anyone else, we were just reaching for our piece of the American Dream.

And my mother made sure that I put my best foot forward, to show the world that we took pride in ourselves and expected, in return, to be treated with respect. I always had a clean shirt and pressed pants for school and good nourishing food in my lunch box. We went to church regularly, where my mother was always making deals with God on our behalf. She promised novenas right and left if He'd make sure we stayed out of trouble, and there were always lots of votive candles burning in her bedroom. As it did among a lot of people with Latin bloodlines, the Catholic Church played a big part in our lives, as a center of the community and a place where people could reconnect with their history and heritage. But at the same time, religion was never something I felt had been imposed on me. My mother seemed happy if I went to Mass once in a while and didn't take the Lord's name in vain. Other than that, I could decide for myself.

She also never raised a hand against me. Well, to be absolutely truthful, there was that one time when she asked me to take out the trash and I flipped her a rude gesture I'd picked up on the street. But other than that, she enforced her discipline with only a stern look and a word of warning.

My sister, Carmen, was another story. If I had to use one word to describe Carmen during those early years it would be "tough." As nails. Like Joey, she was in a street gang, the Galatian Debs, whose turf was the Amsterdam Projects, right around Sixty-second Street before they tore it all down to make way for Lincoln Center. I don't know if God heard all my mother's prayers on behalf of her daughter, but if He did, He wasn't paying much attention. The Debs were the baddest girl gang in the whole of Harlem, worse, in my book, than any of the guys' gangs. They would cruise up and down Amsterdam Avenue popping gum and daring anyone to cross into their territory.

My sister was the leader of the gang and had a special way of handling herself in a fight. I'll never forget the time she was ambushed by two girls from a rival gang in a knock-down-drag-out alley fight. The girls' first line of attack was to go for Carmen's hair, which was exactly what she expected. So she had strategically placed razor blades in her hair before ratting it into the high bouffant that was the style in those days. Needless to say, she walked away with her hairdo barely mussed.

She had the same kind of take-no-prisoners attitude when it came to me. Once, when I'd done something that really pushed her buttons, she grabbed a butcher knife off the kitchen table and chased me around the apartment threatening to cut off . . . well, you get the idea.

As time went on, the family started to wonder if my mother would ever get married again. I'm not sure whether she'd decided one way or the other, even after the divorce from my father became final, but I do know she didn't have the best luck when it came to men.

That incident with Carmen and the butcher knife reminds me of another tense moment in the family kitchen, when my mother brought a man home for a cup of coffee after a night on the town. I woke up hearing the sound of raised voices and, slipping out of bed, peeked around the hallway. I could see my mother and this stranger having an increasingly loud argument, and while I wasn't sure what the problem was, I knew from my mother's tone of voice that she wasn't going to put up with too much more of it.

She stood up, pointing to the door, ordered the man out of the house. He barged past her into the living room and she followed, yelling all the way. I hurried down the hallway and into the kitchen where I could see the two cups of coffee with steam still rising from them and that same knife my sister had pulled on me, resting on a cutting board beside a loaf of bread.

Suddenly from the living room I heard a loud slap and a shriek and looked through the door in time to see that man raise his hand to slap my mother again. There was a lot more yelling, as other members of the house were roused from their sleep, but my only reflex was to grab that knife and protect my mother.

I stood in the kitchen listening as the argument continued, alternately in Spanish and English, the long blade trembling in my hand. Finally, swearing and shouting, the man stomped out of the apartment, slamming the door behind him. I don't know what I would have done if he'd hit my mother again. I was scared and angry all at the same time, but I can still remember the feeling of wanting to protect my mother, to hurt that bad man and make him go away. It was a scary night for any six-year-old kid and I think it was the first time I really understood how vulnerable and exposed we were without a husband and father around to protect us.

But my mother was a good-looking woman, still young and high-spirited, and although I think she never really trusted men after my father's desertion, she still entertained the possibility of romance. I sometimes wonder if she still secretly kept a flame burning for the man she married as a sixteen-year-old country girl, and though I've never put the question to her directly, I suspect that she did. She was the kind of person for whom commitment came naturally. Once she had given her heart to someone, it just wasn't ever going to be available again.

Despite that frightening first date, there was a part of me that really wished my mother would find someone else . . . someone I could call my dad. Papa Don Pino was wonderful, but he was old and set in his old-country ways. I was beginning to notice the difference between having a grandfather who liked to take a nap in his easy chair after dinner and a father who could wrestle you on the living-room floor or take you to a ball game on Saturday afternoon.

It was a distinction that really hit home when I'd be out on the street playing stickball or Johnny-ride-the-pony or ring-a-levio with the neighborhood kids. It would get to be around twilight and we'd be going at the game hot and heavy when someone's father would come around the corner on his way home from work and call out to his kid, "Hey, come on upstairs with me. It's dinner time!" And the kid would stop right in the middle of a swing and run up to get a hug from his old man. He would just forget about the game because he was so happy to see his father and so excited to tell him all the things that had happened since they'd sat around the breakfast table that morning.

More times than not, that scene would repeat itself until I was left standing out on the street by myself as dusk turned to darkness, just thinking about my friends and their families, all together, mom and dad and kids, like it should be. And then my own mother would call from out the window and break that melancholy spell. I'd run home, too, leaving behind that feeling that something was missing . . . at least for a little while.

To be fair, one or two of my mom's boyfriends would try to step into the role of father when they got a chance or the family mood hit them. One guy took me a few times to see Mickey Mantle and the Yankees play. Back then the Yankees were all but unbeatable, but this guy, a real dapper gambler with a sharkskin suit and a handkerchief in his breast pocket, always placed a bet on the opposing team. It bothered me so much that one time I blurted out, "I don't know why you're wasting your money. No one can beat the Yankees." He looked at me and laughed. "You know what, kid?" he said. "You're probably right."

But like my mother's other boyfriends, he stopped coming around after a while and I was left to nurse that empty feeling by myself.

At times like that I looked for comfort where I could, taking on Joey, who, by now, my mom had all but adopted, as a surrogate big brother and even occasional dad.

Eventually, Joey, who'd never quite gotten around to moving back with his own family, was more or less a full-fledged member of the household. He turned out to be a really nice guy once you got past all the macho posturing. Even though he was ten years older than I was we would hang out together, making big plans to take a trip around the world when we grew up.

But the guy who really came the closest, and tried the hardest, to filling the role of father in my life was a good-natured Greek cop by the name of Pete Panos. He dated my mom for almost four years and even asked her to marry him. But, like all the others, he was never able to help her overcome that mistrust or wounded pride or just plain heartbreak that held her back.

But he tried. I think he truly loved her and did his best to show her how honorable his intentions really were. It was always a special day when Pete pulled up in his big white Cadillac convertible and we all piled in for a trip to Jones Beach, complete with ice cream and pony rides.

Even more special was when he'd take me along with him to the police shooting range in Central Park and let me watch him fire off round after round at those paper targets picturing menacing crooks. It was because of Pete Panos that I formed my earliest ambition: When I grew up I wanted to be a cop, just like him. The funny thing is, I almost made it, even if it was only on a television show.

The bond between me and Pete was a link to another way of life, one where a strong man would take charge, protect and serve, just like it said on his shiny badge. I took to pointing him out to my friends as he drove by in the squad car. "That's my stepdad," I would say proudly, hoping that one day it would be more than a white lie I told.

In the meantime, I was getting on with the business of growing up, attending public school for three years. I was forming my first tried-and-true friendships with guys like Leo Ponce, a half–Puerto Rican, half-black kid, and Ronnie Pagliaro, half Italian, half Irish, with milk-white skin, a face full of freckles, and a body so skinny it would hardly make a splash when we'd play hooky to go diving off the docks into the Hudson River.

I guess I cut classes a little too often. When it was time to graduate from the third grade, the principal informed my mother that I'd have to repeat the year because I had been absent so much.

Well, my mother wouldn't hear of it and determined that the fault wasn't mine but the lousy public school system. She made up her mind to put me in Catholic school, a prospect that scared me to death. If the starched uniforms, complete with neckties, weren't enough to put the fear of God into me, then the nuns could finish the job. There was something about those white-and-black habits that spooked me on sight. The image of those faces peering out from their wimples, so pale they seemed to shine, was all I needed to change my ways.

I also had another reason for trying to do better. Her name was Margaret O'Boyle, the prettiest girl at St. Paul the Apostle School, and the first to steal my heart. There have been a lot of women since, a lot of pounding hearts and fluttering eyelashes, but they say you never forget your first love, and for me, little Margaret O'Boyle will always occupy that place of honor.

It was for Margaret's honor that I got into the first fight of my life. I considered her my girlfriend, kind of like a prized possession, and wouldn't stand for anyone giving her a hard time on the playground. Well, there was one kid, Raymond Ferrer, who did just that, teasing and taunting her and making all kinds of lewd suggestions. (Although I'm sure that at our age, he had no idea of what he was actually saying.)

Anyway, I caught wind of this ungentlemanly behavior and confronted Raymond mano a mano. "Margaret is my girlfriend," I said as reasonably as I knew how. "I'd like it if you leave her alone."

"Sure, Henry," he said with a disarming smile. "No problem."

I don't know whether he was afraid of me or just playing for time, but before the day was out I heard through the grapevine that he was promising to kick my butt for my affront to his schoolyard pride. When I heard that, I knew I had to act. That Sunday in church, right after the ten o'clock Mass, I sauntered up to him again.

"I heard you're going to kick my butt," I said casually.

"Yeah? So what?" he said, thrusting out his chin. Before he could say another word I decked him with a roundhouse punch to his glass jaw. He went down like a condemned building and I jumped on top of him. We rolled around in the dust while a crowd of cheering kids gathered.

I think the thing that offended my youthful sense of justice the most was the fact that I had come to him first and asked him to back off. Since he'd agreed and then went around bragging about how he could hardly restrain himself from teaching me a lesson I'd never forget, well . . . I felt justified in throwing the first punch. It was an object lesson I carried with me from that day: If you have to fight someone, make sure you've got the element of surprise on your side.

I also learned that talk was cheap. Even though Raymond paraded around outside my apartment building for the rest of the afternoon, muttering threats and promising to get even, he never touched me, or bothered Margaret again. People can huff and puff all they want, but it's the willingness to back up what you say that counts. It was a little slice of wisdom that would come in very handy later on in Hollywood.

Even though I eventually did have to repeat the third grade, I really turned myself around under the stern gaze of those sisters, excelling especially in math. I discovered that I liked numbers, how they matched up and made sense in a way that real life rarely did.

Real life had already taken a couple of sharp turns. While I was still in public school my mother had been forced to apply for welfare to keep the family fed and clothed, and when new public housing opened up on Amsterdam Avenue, she qualified for an apartment. We had left Papa Dom Pino and the whole unruly crowd behind at the old place on 103rd Street, but it wasn't long before they moved out as well, to a better flat in a better neighborhood on Eighty-eighth Street.

The clan was growing by leaps and bounds, aided by my grandmother's relentless efforts to get her daughters all married off. In the new Eighty-eighth Street digs, they had to make room for my aunt Lucy and her new husband, Joe, who had a good job as headwaiter on a cruise ship. He'd be gone for months at a time but somehow still found time to sire two little girls, Diana and Joanna.

Soon more cousins were showing up from Puerto Rico, including Luco, who was half deaf and spoke in sign language. Uncle Frankie, who was training to be a goldsmith, still needed a place to stay. Also included were Aunt Hattie and Uncle Edwin. (Years later, he would die of Hansen's disease.) Looking back on it, I'd say we got out just in time.

As much as it rocked my little world to be separated from Papa Don Pino, I never really got the chance to miss him. Almost every weekend, my mother would park me with the family on Eighty-eighth Street while she went to work. In those days she had all kinds of different jobs, occasionally working all of them at the same time.

A few of the occupations weren't all that respectable for a Catholic girl. But with two kids to provide for, three if you counted Joey, she did what she had to. Aside from her regular trade as a seamstress, she worked as an exotic dancer in the floor show at one of the big old Latin movie palaces on 125th Street. She wasn't a stripper exactly, but she wore some pretty skimpy outfits, and guys in the audience would just go crazy. She took me to see her dance only once, which was enough for me. I think if I'd had the knife from our kitchen, I would have made mincemeat of the whole matinee audience.

Mom also earned a little pocket money working as an extra in Spanish language TV shows that were shot in New York. As time went on, and she became more and more self-sufficient, the prospect of marriage just faded away. She was making her way on her own and taking care of her family. I think she must have asked herself what any man, even a guy like Pete Panos, could really do for her that she couldn't do for herself. I've got to admit, it was a good question, even though there were plenty of times I wished she'd slow down a little and quit burning the candle at both ends.

Actually, it was more like a firecracker than a candle. My mother had a fierce determination to do things her way, and once she made up her mind nothing could change it. A lot of that stubborn independence, that same unwillingness to compromise, got passed down to me. I can't say that I'm not grateful for the strong character traits I got from her. I sometimes wonder though, if her hard-driving, and hardheaded, way of life might not have been tempered by the love and support of a husband.

One of the values she drilled into me every chance she got was to make my own way, without asking anyone else's help. I remember once heading downtown on a Saturday afternoon to hang out at Herald Square and windowshop at Macy's. When it got late and time to go home I realized that instead of the fifteen-cent subway fare, I had only a dime. As I was standing there wondering what to do, I saw a bum come up to a businessman and ask for spare change. The guy actually dug into his pocket and pulled out a quarter.

For one split second I thought of doing the same thing. I thought maybe I could pick some kindly-looking face out of the crowd and beg for a nickel to get back home. But I just couldn't do it. It was like I could hear my mother inside my head, telling me in that no-nonsense tone of voice she reserved for serious lectures that I was never to ask anyone for anything that I hadn't worked for. I ended up walking the thirty-odd blocks back home, promising myself the whole way that if I could help it, I would never be without enough money in my pockets again.

But until I was old enough to start paying my own way, my mother made sure I never went without. Whatever I saw on that old black-and-white TV that my grandparents had bought for Papa Don Pino to watch the Sunday night fights, my mom made sure I got it. When I had to have a bike one Christmas she saw to it that there was one under the tree, even though she had to buy it from a neighborhood kid and get my grandfather to slap on a new coat of paint. Ice skates, a toy six-gun and holster, it didn't matter. If it was up to her, my childhood was going to be a happy one.

But there are some things you can't give to kids, no matter how hard you try, just like there are some things you can't hide from them. When the time comes to face the hard realities of life and death, all you can do is stand back and let it happen and hope that time will heal the wounds of a young heart.

I can still vividly recall every detail of the night Papa Don Pino died. I can still smell the delicious aroma of the dinner my grand-mother had cooked—rice and beans, fried plantains, and pork chops so moist and delicious we all sat around the table noisily sucking the marrow from the bone. I can hear the muffled sound of the boxing match on TV and see my grandfather sitting in his favorite chair, his calloused hands folded across his big belly. It was an eve-ning like so many others I had spent with them, sleeping over while my mother worked the late shift at the theater.

But this night was going to be different. I knew something was up when my grandmother came in from the kitchen and started scolding Papa Don Pino for sitting in front of the TV. "The doctor said you should get more exercise," she said, shaking her finger at him. "You got to go out for a walk."

I had no idea that my grandfather's health had been slowly declining for years. Back then, of course, no one was making the connection, least of all my old-fashioned grandmother, between all that rich food she was serving him and the way he always seemed to be a little short of breath and red in the face.

And Papa Don Pino wasn't about to start changing his ways. He waved off his wife with a dismissive gesture. "You're standing in front of the picture," he said. "I'm missing the fight."

But my grandmother could be every bit as stubborn as he was. "The doctor says you got to walk," she insisted.

He snorted. "I'm not gonna die until I see Papo's kids," he replied, ruffling my hair and smiling at me in that special way that only we shared.

And that was that. My grandmother was one tough customer, a woman who smoked Chesterfields and put them out on her tongue, but she was no match for Don Pino. After throwing up her arms and muttering some dark Spanish hexes under her breath, she retreated to the kitchen.

If I knew, deep down, that something was wrong, it was confirmed for me later that night. The subtle undercurrent of worry that hung in the house like the smell of that strong coffee they drank with dessert, lingered until I was sent to bed. Instead of putting me to sleep, like always, in my grandfather's room, my grandmother took me to Aunt Haydee's bed. When I asked her why I couldn't sleep with Papa Don Pino she just crossed herself, gave me a kiss, and tried to hide the worried expression on her face.

It must have been after midnight when I was awakened by someone calling my name. The voice sounded strange, far away and full of pain, and I didn't recognize it right away. But the voice kept up, forlornly calling, "Papo . . . Papo . . ." so I slipped out from beside my aunt and crept down the dark hallway, my heart pounding against my ribs.

It was outside his bedroom that I found Papa Don Pino, curled naked on the floor, his big body looking white and helpless in the dim light coming through the window. "Papo," he wheezed. "Get Mama. Go get Mama."

I ran to my grandmother's bedroom, shaking her awake and leading her to the hallway, where my grandfather still lay, his legs crumpled under him by the stroke he had suffered.

After that, the memories become a nightmarish blur of my grandmother's shrieks and sobs, someone frantically calling for help on the phone, and my aunt shooing me away from the sight of my poor grandfather. Then came the long and agonizing wait for the ambulance, a pounding at the door, and a muffled struggle to get my grandfather's limp body onto a gurney.

By morning he was dead. A strong man struck down before his time, he left behind a little boy who, no matter how much they tried to explain, couldn't quite believe that his Papa Don Pino wasn't ever coming back.

Chapter Three

With the death of my grandfather came the end of my childhood, at least the innocence and simple trust that every kid has at one time. To say that I didn't realize how much he meant to me until he was gone doesn't come close to describing the loss I felt. Because I knew exactly what he meant to me, how important he was to the equilibrium of my life. Which is why, when he was alive, I clung to him so tightly and why, when he died, I knew that the world had changed forever.

But, as they say, life goes on, and with it come the ways of coping with loss and loneliness. For me, it was as if, almost overnight, I went from being protected to being a protector, from needing to providing.

The feeling that, in some very real way, my boyhood was over forever came home to me in no uncertain terms shortly after Don Pino's death. As a child I had often begged him to open up an old trunk that he had stashed under his bed. With a sly look and a twinkle in his eye he would lift the top and show me his stash of gold coins, watches, bracelets, and rings . . . a treasure he'd been hoarding since his days on the sugarcane farm.

I'd stare at that bounty with my mouth wide open while he'd

whisper in my ear that he had been saving it all up for me and that, one day, the treasure would be mine.

After his death and funeral, we had the traditional wake, with the family sitting in the living room while friends and neighbors came by to pay their respects. Everyone was talking in hushed and reverent tones while the novenas were said, so no one noticed when I slipped off by myself to the bedroom to claim the inheritance my grandfather had promised me. But when I knelt down to look under the bed, the chest was gone. As I sat alone in that dim room, surrounded by all the familiar objects that comprised my grandfather's life, I think I realized that the dreams and fantasies that we shared were just that—stories that faded away when the storyteller was gone.

With the death of the patriarch, it seemed as if the family itself began to scatter to the four winds. Pretty soon it was just Aunt Lucy and my grandmother, rattling around in the Eighty-eighth Street place, and it wasn't long before they started renting out rooms to Cuban immigrants to bring in some extra money.

My grandmother was in her early sixties when Don Pino died and would go on to live nearly another forty years, as tough at ninety-seven as she was the day she stepped off the boat from Puerto Rico. She worked a steady job sewing in a sweatshop and didn't seem to have the slightest trouble taking care of herself, but now that she was a widow, the family thought it best if she had some extra help around the house.

I was twelve years old when I moved in with my grandmother, running errands for her and sleeping in my grandfather's old room. I stayed with her for a year and a half until she decided that, all things considered, America wasn't all it was cracked up to be and made up her mind to move back to Puerto Rico.

That was fine with me. The simple truth was, I was beginning to break away from the family myself. I had big ambitions for the future, and living with my grandmother in that musty old room with the ghost of Papa Don Pino didn't exactly figure into my plans.

Thanks to the influence of Pete Panos, the notion of becoming a policeman had become more and more appealing. The uniform, the gun, the respect that was automatically yours when you walked down the street—those were just the sort of job benefits that could attract a fatherless young teenager.

Back then, there was one sure way to increase your odds of getting on the force and that was by attending a Catholic school called Powell Memorial Academy down on Sixtieth Street. A long line of New York's finest had graduated from Powell, which had a strong Irish emphasis in its student body. But, thanks to some timely intervention from Pete, I was accepted as a high school freshman.

I knew that attending Powell Academy, which was staffed by Franciscan brothers, was a rare opportunity for a Puerto Rican kid from the projects, and I was determined to make the best of it. But when I took a look at the curriculum requirements I realized I'd be playing catch-up right from the start. Every class required a special textbook, and every one of them was going to cost more than my mother could afford. If I was going to have a prayer of making it in this competitive new school, I was going to have to come up with a way to buy those books.

So I started asking around for a summer job. A neighborhood friend named John Murray came to my rescue. Maybe he was impressed that I'd be going to a school filled with his fellow Irishmen, or maybe he just figured I'd have to work hard if I was going to save all that money. Whatever the reason, he put in a good word with his father, who owned a Laundromat on Amsterdam Avenue, and I was hired to wash the customers' loads for $1.25 an hour.

I worked hard that summer. By the time they opened the doors at Powell, I was the first one to walk through, proudly carrying my new books past those framed pictures of NYPD captains who had graduated with honors. I was going to make it, too, and maybe one day my picture would also be up there, showing off all my polished buttons and gold braid.

Well, it didn't exactly work out that way. I hadn't been there more than a semester, and doing pretty well, I might add, when I went to my locker between classes one day, only to discover that someone had broken in and stolen all my precious schoolbooks.

At that point I could have done one of two things. I could have calmly walked into the office and reported the theft, trusting that whoever had done the deed would be caught or, better yet, feel so guilty that he'd turn himself in. Or I could have gone ballistic.

I chose the second option. Swearing a blue streak, I stormed into the headmaster's inner sanctum, demanding to know how he could allow something like this to happen in a Catholic school in broad daylight. If he had an explanation, I must not have been too interested in hearing it, because I just kept yelling and cursing until they finally called my mother to come down and take control of her wild kid.

By the time she showed up, I was storming down the halls and bursting into classrooms, demanding to know who had snatched my books. As angry as I was, more than anything else I knew this was going to be a fatal setback in my plans for becoming a cop. Powell was one tough school. As hard as I had worked at that Laundromat to buy those books, I worked that much harder to learn what was inside of them. I'd even taken to staying after school for tutoring, trying to crack the secrets of algebra. Now I saw all my efforts going up in smoke.

And that smoke was coming right out my ears. Losing my temper, swearing at those shocked Franciscans, and generally raising holy hell was certainly not the way to get what I wanted. But I just didn't know any better. When you get hit, you hit back. When someone does you wrong, you get even. That's what I thought being a man was all about.

The staff of Powell Academy, it turned out, had different ideas. My outrageous conduct, they told my mother, would force them to reevaluate my suitability for attending their institution, or some such double-talk. My mother, on the other hand, read between the lines right away. I was going to be tossed out on my ear, and the prospect of such a disgrace was more than she could bear. She broke down and started crying, right there in the office.

Well, that was all I needed. Still shouting every four-letter word I could think of, I grabbed my mother's hand and stormed out of the hallowed halls of Powell Academy. I stomped down the street a few blocks to the nearest public school, pushed through the doors, and demanded they enroll me then and there.

The school turned out to be Commerce, one of the most notorious havens for gangs and delinquency in all of New York City. I didn't care. I was going to show them all, and if my mother had any doubts she kept them to herself after seeing the look in my eyes. It must have been familiar to her. It was the same glint of steely determination that she'd greeted the world with her whole life, and she wasn't about to tell me to back off, calm down, and think this through.

Because I'd come from such a prestigious school as Powell, I immediately found my way onto the Honor Roll at Commerce. It was a distinction that didn't last too long. I was still determined to be a policeman, but once the easy access provided by Powell was closed to me, I wasn't sure what my next move was going to be.

It turned out to be in the general direction of down. My stay on the Honor Roll lasted until the end of my freshman year. By the time I returned for my sophomore stint, this time to Brandeis, which was the parent school of Commerce, my academic ambitions pretty much played second fiddle to other concerns. I took to cutting classes again and even had a hard time showing up for band practice after I had taken up the clarinet.

Most of my energies went into making money. I'd held on to my job at the Laundromat, so most afternoons when I should have been studying I was keeping those washers and dryers full—$1.25 an hour for loading, washing, and drying, and a dime extra for bleach.

In between hauling loads of other people's dirty laundry and figuring ways to stay out of school, I developed another moneymaking scheme with a friend of mine from the projects who went by the name of Kingfish. He and I would go down to the Port Authority Bus Terminal on Forty-second Street and buy a bundle of newspapers for a nickel each. We'd then go out hawking them in the bars along Ninth Avenue, from Times Square all the way to Needle Park on Seventy-third and Broadway.

The whole point was to find customers who were either drunk or well on their way, and then perform a little sleight-of-hand when we gave them back their change. Fridays and Saturdays were our best days, with guys already drinking away their paychecks. Some of them were so bombed they hardly noticed when we gave them back a nickel's change for a quarter. Sometimes we even boldly pocketed all the coins while they went back to their whiskey and beer chasers, trying to focus on the paper they'd just bought at premium prices.

When I wasn't selling newspapers, I had a part-time gig delivering prescriptions for a drugstore on Seventy-eighth and Broadway. I had a Raleigh bike at the time, red with small tires, that was more or less an extension of my body. I could hop curbs, jump side walls, and do a three-sixty with grace and poise.

A few blocks down from the drugstore was a beauty shop owned by a couple of my mother's Cuban friends. After I finished my deliveries I would pedal over there and spend a few hours sweeping up the place to earn a couple of extra dollars. By that time it would be getting on toward 7:30—dinnertime—so I'd head directly home.

On Friday nights I would stop over at a florist on Seventy-second Street to buy my mother a dozen roses.

Whatever money I had left after pitching in my share of the family budget went to my wardrobe. I always liked a sharp dresser, since back in the days when I went to Yankee Stadium with that dapper gambler, and I did my best to keep up with the current fashions. At that time, in the mid-sixties, the rage was all Beatle-inspired: corduroy, striped T-shirts, collarless jackets—the whole Merseybeat look. Sometimes the grooviest new threads were just more than I could afford, but I was good at improvising, like during the period when everyone had to have those low-slung Beatle boots. No way was I going to walk into a shoe store with enough cash to own a pair, so what I did was simply cut the tops off a pair of winklepickers I had and, presto!—genuine Fab Four footwear.

Of course, money wasn't the only thing on my adolescent mind and by the time I hit my last two years in high school, I had developed a very healthy obsession with girls. And number one on my hit parade of fantasies was a dynamite strawberry blonde named Christine LaPorte.

It was Christine who sparked my first casual interest in acting. Well, that's not strictly true. My interest was in Christine, who just happened to be in the high school drama club. So, as much as anything, I joined up to stay close to her.

The drama teacher was a very sharp and sophisticated woman named Rita Broadly. Because of her careful enunciation and proper use of English, I was convinced she was a graduate of the Royal Academy or something equally prestigious. I'll forever be grateful for the encouragement she gave me in that class.

On my first day there she asked me why I wanted to act. Since I couldn't very well say that I wanted to do what Christine was doing,

I looked her right in the eye and said, "I've been acting all my life." It was true in a way. Street life demanded that you played all kinds of roles, from tough to timid, depending on the situation. The only difference I could see was that I'd be acting in front of an audience, and that prospect, to tell the truth, made me more than a little nervous.

But Miss Broadly reassured me and that same afternoon gave me an improvisation piece to perform with Christine. For that alone I owed her big time, but as I started getting into the role, taking off on a popular song of the time, "Ode to Billie Joe," I started to realize that I enjoyed the chance to step into another life, take on a new personality, and try to convince everyone that I really was who I pretended to be.

I guess the teacher picked up on my natural affinity for the stage because she took me aside afterward and told me that I had real promise, and that there was a place in her class for me if I wanted it. I did, and not just because of Christine. It was a realization that left me a little surprised at myself. I guess I was still holding on to the idea of being a cop and couldn't quite figure out what acting might have to do with my future.

I had always loved going to the movies, mostly on Saturday afternoons after our newspaper runs up Ninth Avenue. There was nothing like settling into that dark, cool theater with a hot dog, popcorn, and a soda spread out around you, ready to get carried away by the flickering images on the big screen. I went in mostly for double features and liked horror movies, especially if Vincent Price was in them. My two favorites were *The Tingler* and *House on Haunted Hill*.

But my all-time favorite actor was John Garfield and I never missed a movie when his name was on the marquee. He was smooth and suave and had all the right moves, but at the same time, his face on the screen seemed so remote and far away it was like watching a god take on human form. It never occurred to me that real people acted in the movies.

Whatever I missed in the theaters I ended up watching on *The Million Dollar Movie*, which aired on Channel 9. The program ran the same show twice a night, so if you didn't see it the first time you could still catch it. It was on TV that I was first introduced to Hollywood legends from Bogart and Cagney to Cary Grant and Gary Cooper. Even though their oversized personalities were reduced to fit onto that small screen, there was still something larger-than-life in those faces, a mysterious magnetism that drew me in and kept me spellbound. It was the same feeling I got when I worked at a dry cleaner's down on Sixty-seventh Street, across the street from ABC-TV. There I'd see all the stars of *As the World Turns* and *All My Children* coming and going. Later, if I happened to catch them on one of the shows, it was hard at first to make the connection between the real flesh-and-blood person and the glamorous image shimmering on the screen.

Girls, on the other hand, were a little bit too real for me to handle sometimes. As I started growing into my teenage frame, making it past the gawky stage, I had a steady string of quasi-steady girlfriends through my junior and senior years. The funny thing is, almost none of them were Puerto Rican or even Latino.

I mostly seemed to attract Jewish girls, and I'm not sure why, except that maybe I represented some kind of forbidden fruit. I know that's how their dads looked at me, because I could see it in their faces when I came to pick their daughters up for a date. I was every inch the sharp-looking street kid and not at all the kind of prospect they were hoping for for their precious little girls. I can't say that I blame them. If I had a daughter and someone looking like I did showed up at the front door, I'd probably lock her in a closet.

The parental response got particularly tense with one girl, Denise. She had the hair and face, if not quite the body, of a young Raquel

Welch; in short, she was just my type. Unfortunately, I wasn't exactly her old man's type and he flat out refused to let her go out with me. I had to be content with secret meetings, just like a scene out of *West Side Story*.

The famous Broadway musical was, in fact, a real romantic touchstone for me. Some of the scenes for the movie had been shot in the playground right across the street from the Amsterdam projects when I was thirteen and I'd hung around all day watching them. It was only when they started dancing that I lost interest. But for a lovesick teenager, that whole cross-cultural Romeo-and-Juliet routine really struck a chord. I felt just like Tony, deprived of his one true love by a society that didn't understand.

But I got over it, mending my broken heart on a bench in Central Park, making out with girls who were only too happy to help me forget Denise. And every one of them was an expert at taking a guy right to the brink without actually "going all the way."

When I finally did lose my virginity, it wasn't to any one of those high school sweethearts. Instead it was at the practiced hands of the proverbial "older woman."

The truth is, there was a lot about her that was pretty mysterious, and she seemed to like it that way. Looking back, my best guess is that she was some sort of high-priced call girl. She was a beautiful woman with finely chiseled features, a haughty, Hamptons-bred air, and a body that just wouldn't quit.

The first time I met her was when I was still at the Laundromat and she came in to have her clothes washed and dried. I couldn't help noticing all the skimpy lingerie that came with her load, real silk and really sexy. After she gave me strict instructions about how to handle her delicate undergarments, she gave me her address—a swank apartment down on Forty-third Street—and asked me to deliver her clean laundry. Personally.

Well, the first couple of times we played this little charade all I got was a heavy tip. But the third time I knocked on the door she answered it stark naked. I had no idea what to do next, except pick my chin up off the floor after she invited me in. We were just getting comfortable when she asked me how old I was.

When I told her my age, she visibly stiffened. She hadn't counted on my being underage and she quickly showed me out.

But I guess once she got the notion in her head, she couldn't rest until she got what she wanted . . . and what she wanted was me. She dropped by the Laundromat a few days later and casually asked me if I'd like to go with her to a movie. I didn't see why not and, to be honest, she wasn't the only one who had a notion stuck in her head. My palms would sweat every time she came through the front door of the Laundromat.

The inevitable upshot was that she overcame her reluctance and took me to bed with her. They say you never forget your first time and it's true, but what I remember best is the way she took a sort of maternal interest in me afterward. She was, after all, almost old enough to be my mother, and whenever I'd come up to her place for a "delivery" she'd ask me about my plans for the future, as smoke rose lazily from the cigarette she always lit up right after we made love.

She encouraged me to continue my education, go to college and get a degree, but mostly she urged me to start saving my money. She was smart that way and I knew it just by looking around her lavishly decorated lair. However she got her money, she knew what to do with it once she earned it.

*   *   *

So I went along with her when she suggested that we go down to her bank so I could open a savings account. I had never actually done anything as grown-up as opening my own account and I was visibly nervous when the bank officer started asking me questions.

"Occupation?" he said.

I was so nervous that, even though I knew exactly what he meant, I blurted out "Puerto Rican . . ." I'll never forget the look he gave me. I felt so stupid, way out of my league, and like nothing more than her pet stud, without a brain in my head.

That was enough for me. I turned on my heel and walked out of the bank without looking back, determined that I wasn't going to let myself be used again—by anybody.

Chapter Four

Considering where I came from, the kind of neighborhood I grew up in, and the kind of role models I had around me, it may seem strange that I didn't get myself into more trouble during those tumultuous teenage years.

The way I look at it, if you see poverty and crime, drugs and despair, around you every day, you've got one of two choices. You can either give up or get out. And for me, there was never any option. I had things to do and something to prove. Maybe that singlemindedness was also a response to being left without a father. The only thing I knew was that, no matter what, I wasn't going to end up like him. He remained confined to a wheelchair, a haunted look in his hollow eyes.

Sure, I had my run-ins with petty crime. I'd broken into a couple of phone booths for the handful of dimes that tumbled out and, when I was little, stole some tin-plated toys from the Woolworth on 105th Street and Second Avenue. The first day I got away with it, but the second time the clerk caught me and spared no detail in describing how I'd go straight to jail if I ever showed my face around there again. I remember running all the way home in a blind panic, racing up the stairs and throwing the toys I had hidden at the bottom of a drawer right out the window. That was the last time I ever took something that didn't belong to me, even though there would be plenty of people who would accuse me of exactly that later in my career.

For me, the idea of hanging out with a gang to try to prove you were a man was just a waste of time. Real men had nice clothes and money in their pockets, and I'd promised myself back down in Herald Square that I'd never again be without a pocket full of change. I liked money, liked the heavy feel of it next to my thigh and the way it jingled as I walked. And when I got a little older I liked the feel of a thick wad of bills in my hip pocket just as much. That's what mattered to me, more than some macho code that could get you killed. Sure, I could have made money in a gang, but I might not have lived long enough to enjoy it.

Which isn't to say that I didn't have my own crew of loyal friends to roam the streets with me. We may not have had a gang name or colors, but we were a bad bunch of dudes. The brothers Gary and Billy Rivera, my grade-school buddy Leo Ponce, Ronnie Pagliaro, and a couple of other hangers-on and I made a real renegade mix of ragtag homeboys—blacks, Puerto Ricans, Italian, and Irish who knew New York like the backs of our hands.

We could have more fun in one day at Coney Island, eating hot dogs and riding the Cyclone, than any other army of kids could have in a week, especially that one Easter when I took the money my mother gave me to buy a new suit and treated my pals to a day at the amusement park.

Another favorite waste of time was to hang out at the piers on Forty-fourth Street, where we'd discovered a wholesale bakery. We'd wait all afternoon until they threw out the baked goods that hadn't sold and gorge ourselves on day-old doughnuts and crullers.

But I think the real reason I made sure to keep my nose clean was the continuing influence of Pete Panos, the Greek cop who kept an eye on the family even after he stopped dating my mom.

Pete worked for a while as a police photographer and sometimes he brought crime scene snapshots for me to see. It was a close-up look at the real price of crime, and I'm sure that's exactly what he wanted to impress upon me: battered and abused women, young punks with slashed throats and bullet-riddled bodies, corpses sprawled on the sidewalk like bloodsoaked rag dolls. I got the message.

But more than scaring me straight, Pete set an example for me. He was a good cop, loved and respected in the neighborhood, and it was from him that I learned that a policeman's real job wasn't to arrest the bad guys. It was to help the people who needed help, the defenseless citizens who couldn't fend for themselves.

There were things happening in the mid-sixties, however—changes and questions and challenges to the status quo—that nobody could defend against. It was just in the air, this feeling that the old way of doing things, the values and morals and safe assumptions of the whole society, were totally up for grabs. It may have started out in San Francisco, but by the time the hippie counterculture swept over East Harlem, I was more than ready to give it a try.

I spent the summer between my junior and senior years in high school hanging out in Greenwich Village. I made a few friends down there, free spirits who were dabbling in drugs and invited me along for the trip.

At first it was a lot of fun. We would rendezvous on a Friday or Saturday night at MacDougal and Bleecker streets, or on a Sunday afternoon in Washington Square, and they'd give me part of a pill or whatever else they had on hand, and we'd all wander around in a blissed-out daze. It seemed like you could hear the Beatles or the Rolling Stones playing out of every open window, but my personal favorites were The Rascals, local boys who made good with songs that really captured that place and time, like "Good Lovin'" and "Groovin'."

There were some really cute girls down in the Village and they all seemed to buy into the "free love" line that was so much a part of the hippie credo. But what really turned them on was a few tokes from a joint, and I could understand why. The few times I smoked marijuana I felt light as a feather and free as a bird, floating down the street, caught up in all the pretty colors and just happy to be alive.

I remember more than a few times coming home to the projects, singing to myself and heading straight for the refrigerator, where I'd satisfy a raging case of the munchies by eating everything. The world seemed especially good that summer, full of adventure and romance and intrigue, and I was beginning to think that the life of a free spirit suited me well.

Pete Panos and my mom, on the other hand, had different ideas. I only found out later how concerned they really were that I was being lured away into a life of decadence and drug addiction. There were times when they actually followed me down to the Village, Pete using all his police training to trail me, and it's a wonder I never noticed that big white Caddy lumbering down the street behind me. Whenever they saw me duck into some disreputable dive like The Bitter End for a night of jazz or a local coffeehouse for a potent cup of espresso, Pete would want to jump out of the car and haul me back home. "Let him go," my mom would say. "Let him find his own way."

And eventually I did. I stopped smoking pot after one disastrous date when, after sharing a joint, all I could do was laugh: I'd laugh because I was laughing and laugh because I was thinking about laughing and laugh because I couldn't stop laughing, and all my poor date could do was just stare at me and wonder where I'd left my marbles.

But the real turning point came when I hooked up with a gorgeous hippie girl named Erica. We were quite a couple: Hank and Erica, she with that long black hair she used to iron straight and I in my sandals, Beatle bangs, and wide-wale corduroy. We'd spend hours together roaming the back streets of the Village and Little Italy, or hanging out under the arch in Washington Square, which was ground zero for the world of New York flower power.

That whole block was really our own little kingdom, with the fountain at its center and all those footpaths branching out to every point on the compass. We had a name for each one of those trails: Junkie Path for the one where the heroin addicts did their business; Family Path, where parents pushed their kids in strollers; and whenever Erica and I met it was always along the tree-lined tributary of Lover's Lane, which was lined with make-out benches.

Erica's parents were teachers at NYU, which was a hotbed of revolution during that time, but whether or not she actually got those sugar cubes of LSD from some inspired chemist in the science department I'll never know. All I know is that when she offered it to me, I didn't think twice. Acid was in the news a lot in those days, with all sorts of controversy swirling around the claims of drug prophets like Timothy Leary, promising that one dose would change your life forever.

I didn't know if I wanted my life changed, but I was willing to try anything once, especially if it was Erica who was asking. Besides, I was a firm believer in the power of my own mind to control anything, convinced that no cube of chemically laced sugar was going to rob me of self-control.

Well, the first three or four hours of that acid trip was like something out of a scene from *Yellow Submarine*: lights and colors and warm, fuzzy feelings for all mankind. I vaguely recall riding around on a city bus, going nowhere in particular and not caring until about two o'clock in the morning when we found ourselves back in the Village. I suddenly realized I was hungry and we headed over to an all-night diner, where I ordered a sausage sandwich piled high with cooked onions. I was munching contentedly when suddenly Erica announced that she had to split.

Walking her to the bus stop, I finished off my sandwich and gave her what must have been a very fragrant kiss good night. Alone now, I doubled back along Fourth Street and into what suddenly seemed like the wilderness of Washington Square. Wandering down the walk where the old men gathered to play chess, I looked up and saw the mysterious figure of a girl standing in the circle of a street-light. As I got closer I was horrified to see her face, glimpsed under a thick mat of tangled hair, start to shift and slide as if it were made of melting wax.

"This is just a chemical reaction," I told myself as I got closer. "This is nothing but a hallucination." But hallucination or not, the sight of her face suddenly dissolving into a mass of writhing worms was a little more than I could handle. Every muscle in my body wanted to turn and run from this monstrous vision, but I knew that if I gave in to the terror I'd be losing control of my own reality, so I took a few steps closer to her and, as I did, the worms and melting flesh disappeared to reveal just a homely girl giving me a crooked come-hither smile.

It was only then that I let myself back away. I headed quickly up the path until I was alone, then sat down at a bench to watch the sun come up.

As day broke, the city all around me began to awake and I felt as if I were in a vast grid of electric life surging and sparking all around me. It was an exhilarating feeling, not just to be in the city but to be a part of it, plugged-in to the pulsing energy of all that concentrated humanity. As I sat there, transfixed by all that chemical clarity, the park itself began coming to life, first with the chirping of birds and rustle of foraging squirrels, then with people strolling by, enjoying the sunshine of a perfect Sunday morning.

Everyone looked so beautiful to me, fresh and happy and full of the simple joy of being alive, but it was then that I realized a sense of separation between all these contented citizens and me, a would-be hippie on the tail end of an all-night drug escapade. I looked down at myself, at my dirty, sandaled feet and sweat-stained T-shirt, and a sudden wave of revulsion passed through me. This wasn't who I was, some grubby denizen of the streets, living in the shadows and talking to the hallucinations that bubbled up through my fevered brain. I walked across the park to a store window and looked at my reflection. My hair was long and unkempt and I hadn't shaved in days. It was a grungy image underscored by the last flickering effects of the acid, and in a way, my own reflection was as ugly and distorted as that girl's wormy face in the park.

I hurried down the street, past the picturesque strollers and the bubbling fountain and jumped on the uptown subway at Sixth Avenue. As soon as I got home I took a hot shower and had a close shave and threw my hippie clothes down the incinerator chute. My days as a free spirit were over. I was back where I belonged, in the real world.

As my senior year in high school began to unfold, that world revolved more and more around the drama club I had joined. Our big production for that year was a play called *Dark of the Moon*, and I landed the lead part. The role I was to play was a half-animal, half-man called The Witch Boy who lived on a mountain and fell in love with a beautiful human named Barbara Allen, who was going to be played by Christine LaPorte.

It was a mythic story, full of magic and symbolism, and lots of passionate emotions. I took to it right away. My focus on that play was constant and intense—to the point of letting everything else slide in anticipation of going to rehearsals and putting on that Witch Boy role like a perfectly fitted suit of clothing.

Acting for me was more than a creative outlet. It was a revelation. All my life I had felt this restless urge to express myself, as if I had something hidden inside of me that was aching to come out but couldn't find its way. Onstage I was able to get in touch with that part of myself, to reach inside and pull out feelings and thoughts and aspirations that I'd never been able to name before. It was more than just stepping into a role, it was like stepping into a part of me that was bigger and better and bolder than the Henry Estrada the rest of the world could see. Acting was a release, better than pot or acid or any other drug you can name. It was also like discovering some incredible ability within myself, a skill and inbred talent that felt both strange and familiar, completely natural and totally unique.

As much as I'd gotten into drama class to stay close to Christine, as the year progressed and the play began to take shape, I was now involved for the sheer love of acting. I had pretty much gotten over my crush on Christine and turned my romantic attention to Maggie, a very classy girl from the Upper West Side.

Maggie was an exotic mix of Latino and Jewish and came from an aristocratic Colombian family. My mother fell in love with her immediately, as much for her impeccable manners as her Latin heritage. I'll never forget the first time I had Maggie over to the apartment. My mom was serving refreshments and while I asked for a Coke, Maggie very demurely requested a cup of tea. I burst out laughing; it seemed so out of place in our housing project kitchen, but my mom shut me up right away with a look that shot daggers. Maggie was her kind of girl and, to tell the truth, I was pretty taken with her myself.

The opening night of *Dark of the Moon* drew closer and I wanted everyone I knew to be on hand for my moment of glory, especially Maggie. But when I asked her to come, she begged off, claiming she had to study for a test. My feelings were hurt and I let her know it, but I couldn't change her mind, and even on opening night I caught myself wondering angrily why she wasn't in the audience.

The performance was a big success, with all my friends gathering around me as if I, too, were suddenly a little larger than life, which was exactly how I felt. But even with all the praise and accolades, I couldn't get over my girlfriend's absence, until I saw her step out of the crowd with a shy smile.

I broke away from my admirers and took her to a quiet corner.

"I thought you weren't coming," I said, letting her hear the hurt in my voice.

"I didn't want to," she replied. "But I couldn't help myself. I knew you'd be great."

"But why?" was all I could ask. "Why didn't you want to be here?"

She took my hand and looked deeply into my eyes. "Hank," she said, "I know how you feel about acting. I've known ever since your first rehearsal. I could see it in your eyes. It's the most important thing in your life right now. And that's what I wanted to be."

"That's crazy," I started to say, but she put her hand up to stop my words.

"No, it's not," she answered quietly. "You've always said you wanted to be a policeman, and that's what I want for you, too. Because that's just a job, something you leave behind at the end of the day. Being an actor is a way of life and it's a life that can never include me. I know I'd lose you and I don't want that to happen."

Before that moment, I'd never really thought about what I might be doing for the rest of my life. Acting was fun. Being a cop . . . well, that was a real job. But as she said those words, it was like a switch went off inside of me. I knew she was right, that she could see something I hadn't seen until she held that mirror up to my face.

"Maggie," I said slowly, "I don't want to be a cop anymore. I want to act."

She just nodded. Maggie already knew what my choice was going to be. She'd counted up the cost of that decision and decided that, for her, it was too high a price to pay. She couldn't compete. The call was too strong.

But for me, no price was too high. I'd turned a corner, and for what was maybe the first time in my life, I knew exactly where I wanted to go. The only question remaining was how to get there.

The only person I could go to who might know the answer to that question was my high-school drama teacher, Rita Broadly. Getting advice about my future became more critical as my high school years were drawing to a close and I was told that since I didn't have enough credits to graduate, I'd have to come back for six months the following fall before I could get my diploma.

Returning to school for another six minutes, never mind six months, was the last thing I wanted to do, so I had extra incentive for getting a firm answer from Miss Broadly. After all, if I was going to be an actor, why did I even need to bother with a high school education?

She didn't quite see it that way, at least at first. I was her star pupil and had walked away with the school's drama award for my work in *Dark of the Moon*, but when I told her I wanted to pursue acting as a career she was adamant. "Get your diploma," she urged. "Finish high school. Acting is the toughest profession there is. Get a college education so you'll have something to fall back on in case it doesn't work out."

Not working out wasn't an option I was ready to entertain and I told her so. She tried again to convince me that I needed a fall-back position, but now that I knew what I wanted, nothing was going to stop me from going for it.

I guess she saw that old Cardona determination glinting in my eye, because, after looking around to make sure we were alone, she leaned in close, speaking to me in a soft but serious tone.

"Henry," she said, "In my twenty-three years of teaching drama, a lot of kids have told me they wanted to become actors. There were only two that I ever encouraged to go ahead and chase the dream. Now I guess you'll be the third."

That was just what I wanted to hear, the "all clear" to make it or break it. I smiled broadly and gave her a kiss on the cheek as I headed out the door.

But right at the threshold of that familiar, dimly lit, and musty old auditorium, I stopped and turned back to where she was sitting on the edge of the stage, where I'd spent so many happy hours.

"So," I asked, "what happened to the first two?"

Now it was her turn to smile. "One of them's married with children," she said. "The other one is a shoe salesman."

Chapter Five

Of course, as a million and one failed actors will tell you, the difference between wanting to act and being able to survive while doing it is as long and wide as the distance from Spanish Harlem to Hollywood Hills. The trick, I've learned, is not to think about the mountain you've got to climb to get to the top, but just to put one foot in front of the other. Sooner or later you'll arrive, and if you don't, you'll have learned all the virtues of patience, perseverance, and putting up with rejection.

The first step I had to take after graduating from high school was to tell my mother I was giving up on my lifelong ambition to be a cop. As you might expect, she didn't take the news too well, insisting that acting was no life for any son of hers. Like Miss Broadly, she must have seen that stubborn look on my face, the one I'd learned from her, because she quickly let the subject drop in favor of a more surreptitious approach.

I discovered her plan a few days later when I was walking through the projects and was suddenly cut off by a cop car pulling in front of me right over the curb. Since my mom had dated Pete Panos for all those years, we'd gotten to know virtually every cop in the neighborhood, from the 18th Precinct down to the 24th Precinct. It was obvious what Mom was up to when one of the officers got out of the squad car and pulled me aside. "So, Papo," he said, "how's it going?"

"Okay," I said, wondering what was up. Had they finally caught up with me for that Woolworth heist?

"How's your mom?" the cop continued, his poker face not giving me a clue.

"Okay," I said. "Listen, I should be goin'. I gotta be somewhere."

"Your mom's a very special lady," the cop went on, totally ignoring me.

"Look," I shot back impatiently. "What's this all about, anyway?"

"It would be a shame for anyone to disappoint her," he answered, leaning in close. "It'd be a shame if her only son decided that being a cop like he always said he would wasn't important anymore."

"Hey!" I said, outraged. "What's she been telling you guys?"

"Come on, Hank," said the cop, throwing a big, beefy arm over my shoulder. "You don't want to be no pansy actor. You're a cop . . . one of us."

Well, after this little scene repeated itself a few times I had a showdown with my mom, telling her in no uncertain terms that I'd made up my mind. After that, the cops stopped hassling me, but I did notice a lot more votive candles burning around the apartment.

I guess my mom would have been within her rights to toss me out on the street to express her disapproval, but that's not the kind of person she was. Once I made it clear that my course was set, she offered me the freedom, and even the support, to give acting my best shot. On the other hand, she wasn't about to let me lounge around the apartment all day waiting for agents and producers to make me a star. If I was going to do my own thing, I'd have to do it on my own dime.

Which meant that once I decided I wasn't going back to school,

I had to get a real job, to pay for my room and board. So I picked up a tip from a friend about a restaurant called Yellowfingers, across town near Bloomingdale's, that needed waiters. I landed a part-time gig there while I looked around for a convenient opening into the New York theater world.

As luck would have it, at just about that time New York City was looking for ways to help promote awareness of its multicultural makeup. Mayor Lindsay had helped to fund something called the Hispanic Culture Workshop, part of which was a Hispanic theatrical troupe that would perform at various sites around town.

It was a very sweet deal, even for a kid who wasn't all that connected with his Hispanic roots. Applicants who were accepted into the program got thirty-two dollars a week, a free lunch every day, and training in drama, speech, and dance, including jazz, modern, and ballet.

Naturally, when I heard about it through some acting friends of mine, I hustled down to the auditions, but not before stopping off to see Miss Broadly. Since she was one of the most highly respected drama teachers in the school system, I knew that a good word from her would mean a lot, and, of course, she agreed. My audition was a scene from the boxing drama *Golden Boy,* and when the directors of the program told me I had been accepted, I've got to be honest in saying that I really wasn't surprised. Back then, I had an attitude that more than made up for my lack of experience and know-how. I was going to make it, and since I was absolutely convinced of that fact, it wasn't hard for others to pick up on my self-confidence and start to believe it themselves.

After a few weeks of training, our theater group began its performance schedule, driving way uptown in a flatbed truck to my old neighborhood in Spanish Harlem, setting up a few crude sets, and staging simple shows, mostly revolving around traditional South and Central American folksongs. Since I couldn't speak Spanish I had to sound out most of the lyrics phonetically, but I was nothing if not a quick study. I had the hang of it in no time, even though I wasn't sure exactly what I was supposed to be so soulfully crooning about. The standard costume of the troupe was that of a Mexican campesino—white shirt, pants and shoes, a red sash around the waist with a wooden machete, and a straw sombrero.

Out of forty hopefuls, ten of us were selected for the troupe, which was called Los Muchachos de San Juan, reflecting our primarily Puerto Rican makeup. We'd perform live five nights a week. I think even my mother, who at the time was still on welfare, was impressed when I came home every payday with a bouquet of flowers and half my check to help with the household bills.

When we weren't playing for free on the streets of the barrio, we'd be booked for professional gigs, such as the ritzy Mexican restaurant La Fonda del Sol. We'd stroll by and sing at the tourists' tables, and since I was the tenor, a husband or boyfriend would sometimes single me out and slip me a five to make a fuss over his wife or girlfriend.

Performing was fun, and there did seem to be the real possibility of using the troupe to make a career move if I was smart and ambitious enough. One of the singers who had been there before me had gone on to Broadway in *West Side Story*, and after I was gone the famous Hispanic comedian Freddie Prinze got his start in Los Muchachos de San Juan.

But for the most part, the kids that were in that program didn't take it all that seriously. Many were in college, with careers already staked out, and saw that the chance to sing and act was a good outlet for their creative urges. For them, it was more of a hobby than anything else, and even though they could perform as well as I could, if not better, it wasn't the serious business proposition for them that it was for me. As a result, I never formed any really strong attachments within the troupe. I was after something else, something more, and I think that driving ambition was a little offputting to the rest of those kids. Some of them, like me, were from the wrong side of the tracks, while others had come from families with good business, or even diplomatic, connections to Latin America. But none of them was as hungry as I was.

I stayed with the program for about a year, working part-time at Yellowfingers, but after a second summer rolled into view I realized that dressing up as a peasant and singing on street corners wasn't going to get me where I needed to go. By that time my goal was in sharp focus: the movies.

Maybe it went back to seeing John Garfield up on the screen, exuding that powerful presence and effortless charm. Or maybe it was the fact that he, and all the other great stars of Hollywood, could make it look so easy. Or maybe it was just that I was a cocky kid, sure that once they got a good look at my pearly teeth and dark brown eyes, the rest would be easy. Whatever it was, I was more than ready for my close-up.

Until Hollywood beat a path to my door, however, I had a lot of time to kill. So in the interests of polishing my craft, I enrolled in the American Musical & Dramatic Academy down on Thirty-fourth Street. At the time, the government offered grants to the school for needy students and there was no one needier than me: I just plain needed to succeed. They accepted me on the spot, as much to fill their quota of poor minority students as for any conspicuous talent I might have had on display.

The next two years of my life took on a regular routine which, while it may not have rocketed me to the top, at least helped me feel that I was making some steady, if slow, progress. I was still living at home and still working as a waiter while I studied everything from fencing to dramatic movement to improvisation to mime at the Academy.

One of the most important courses I took was in speech. As a Puerto Rican from Harlem, I had developed what you might call a distinctive accent, and I really had to work hard to get rid of it or risk being typecast as a New York ethnic for the rest of my life.

All the while, I was keeping my eyes and ears open for a chance to get into movies. The late sixties to early seventies was a very active period for filmmaking in New York, with a lot of major production shootings on the city streets. So my first move was to try to get work as an extra, a job that paid the grand total of twenty-seven dollars and fifteen cents a day. There were casting agencies just for extras springing up all over town. I made the rounds, dropping my name anywhere there was a chance it might be picked up, and scanned the entertainment trade papers for news of upcoming New York productions.

But I didn't stop there. I gave a lot of thought to how I could best get a break in films and came up with what I considered an ingenious angle. I realized that the chances of the production companies actually being based in New York were pretty slim. I figured they were coming from California, which meant that they could really benefit from someone who knew the streets and the street attitude you needed to get by in the Big Apple. Chances were, their crews had no idea how to handle the wackos, thugs, and con artists infesting the city. Not to mention the fact that most of the unions in those days were segregated, so there wasn't much chance that they would have blacks or Latinos who could handle their own kind in a crowd. I had it all figured out.

The next day, I showed up at the location for a low-budget film being shot on the streets and singled out the location manager.

I introduced myself in my smoothest and most charming manner, adding, "Remember the name. I'm gonna be an actor."

"Sure you are, kid," said the manager, already losing interest and starting to walk away. He must have heard that line a thousand times before.

"Look," I said, hurrying after him, "I've got a proposition for you."

Something in my cocky attitude caught his attention. He stopped. "Make it quick," he growled. "I'm a busy man."

"I bet you are," I answered, warming up to my pitch. "And you're gonna get busier once this neighborhood finds out there's a movie being made around here."

"Your point being?" I could tell he was getting impatient, but I could also tell he was a little interested in where all this was heading.

"My point is," I continued, "you need someone who knows how to handle the people around here to keep things rolling."

"That's what the cops are for," he said, looking at a long list on his clipboard and no doubt wondering why he was wasting his time with me.

I laughed and he gave me a sharp look. "Hey, don't get me wrong," I said, "but that's really funny. These people don't care about cops. They're New Yorkers. If a cop tells them what to do, they'll do the opposite just to piss him off."

"Yeah, well, I'll take my chances," the manager snorted and started to move off again through the crowded downtown street.

I grabbed him by the arm. Now I was really taking a chance, but it was too late to stop. "You're the boss," I said, "but I just hope that when your boss wants to get his shot, there's not a whole bunch of lowlifes in the background flipping off the camera."

He hesitated. I let go of his arm and stepped back, giving him a chance to think it over. "So what are you proposing, exactly?" he finally asked.

"It's simple," I replied, flashing him my most winning smile. "Anybody comes around here drunk or disorderly, any troublemakers try to get in your way, I'll take care of it." I leaned over, as if I was sharing a special secret, just between him and me. "They'll listen to me," I said. " 'Cause I can talk their language. And all you gotta do is let me watch the actors at work."

He looked me over one more time and grinned. "Okay, kid," he said. "You've got yourself a deal."

A teamster lounging in the cab of his truck called out his name and the manager hurried off. I just stood there for a moment, unable to believe my good luck. But I managed to pull myself together in time to shout after him, "Oh, one last thing."

"What's that?" he said over his shoulder.

"I want to get twenty-seven fifteen a day for my services. Just like a real extra."

One thing I had no lack of back then was cojones.

So I finally had my way in and you better believe I made the most of it. With the threat of unruly citizens, I never really had a problem. Most people were as much in awe of the moviemaking process as I was, and the last thing they'd dream of doing was ruining a shot. But I made sure to look busy patrolling the set, even as I was soaking up all the acting and directing around me.

In the course of those few weeks I got a firsthand education in the technical end of film production: everything from arcs to nine lights; gaffers to best boys. It was exactly what I imagined: fun and exciting and stimulating even when all anyone seemed to be doing was sitting around waiting for the crew to set up the next scene. I had to be a part of this, no matter what.

That first job as a "security agent" quickly turned into others as I continued studying at the Academy and hung out every spare minute on whatever movie set happened to be in town. I was on location for *The Landlord, Cactus Flower, John and Mary*, and a few others. On every set I made sure I got to be on a first-name basis with anyone who'd give me the time of day.

From there it was only a short jump to actually being an extra. I even got to do a little stunt work on a film called *The Out-of-Towners*, directed by Arthur Hiller and starring Jack Lemmon and Sandy Dennis. I'd been hired as an extra, along with Phil Surano, who was also interested in acting and remains one of my best buddies to this day. The scene they were shooting was down on the

West Side at Fifty-seventh Street, near a big old empty warehouse. It called for two stunt doubles to stand in for the leads, and while it didn't require anything more than driving an old '57 Chevy erratically down a ramp, Phil and I grabbed the chance. Later, when the movie came out, I went to see it a half dozen times just for that scene, even though it was so dark and far away you couldn't tell us apart. But I knew. I was the dude driving.

I got my Screen Actors Guild (SAG) card working on *John and Mary*. The scene was in a big auditorium where Dustin Hoffman was trying to talk to a bunch of protesting students. Well, I'd made it a point to get very friendly with a guy named Marty Richards, who did most of the casting of extras for New York City shoots, and the day of the scene he pulled me aside.

"Listen, Hank," he said, "I think I can get you a SAG card from this scene. We'll put you up at the front of the crowd and if you yell really loud, you'll qualify." The SAG rule for membership was that you had to have a speaking part in a film, which meant that if I could make myself heard above the roar, I'd be in. Membership was a big deal since it allowed you to make more money and put you in contention for actual roles. Lots of guys spent years trying to get their card, so you can bet that I screamed myself hoarse when the camera panned that mob. And it worked, which made *John and Mary* another movie I sat through a half dozen times, just to pick out my voice on the soundtrack.

Before too long I was a regular fixture on virtually every movie being shot anywhere in the five boroughs, sometimes working two productions a day, starting at dawn in Grand Central Station and ending up at two in the morning down in my old Village stomping grounds.

I was really working the angles now, getting my portfolio and headshot publicity photos together and dropping them off at agents' offices and on the sets where I worked. I remember personally handing a glossy eight by ten to Joanne Woodward, although I'm sure if

59

you asked her about it, she wouldn't remember that pushy Latin kid accosting her on the set.

I loved the whole highly charged atmosphere that clung to movie sets like the smell of hot lights and makeup and was convinced that it was only a matter of time before I'd get my chance to look straight into the camera and deliver a ringing line of dialogue.

So when that moment finally happened, it seemed less like a dream come true than a sure thing that had just paid off.

Chapter Six

Getting your first big break in the movies feels great for about the first five minutes. That's when all those visions of money, women, and mass adulation dance through your brain; when you start writing your Oscar acceptance speech, posing next to your star on the Hollywood Walk of Fame, and putting your hands in concrete outside Mann's Chinese Theatre.

After that, the panic sets in. You start thinking about what's riding on your performance: millions of dollars, the hard work of dozens of other people, and most of all, your own future. You begin to wonder if you've really got what it takes, if you've been kidding yourself, and everyone else, all along, and if your first big break is also going to be your last. You start imagining your smiling face in the pages of a "Where Are They Now?" article and end up wondering if you could just slip out of town.

Then comes the hard work of rehearsals, long hours on location, dealing with the personalities, and the problems that inevitably arise in the pressure-cooker atmosphere of a motion-picture production. When it's all over, you might find yourself wondering if the roller-coaster ride was worth it after all.

But if you're at all honest with yourself, the answer to that question has got to be, You better believe it.

Simply put, there is nothing more exciting and exhausting, more frustrating and fulfilling, more inspiring and unnerving, than being in the movie business. And each aspect of the job is magnified a thousand times when it's you who's got the star on his trailer, all the best lines, and your name at the bottom of a lot of fine print.

Of course I didn't know about any of that the morning I got a call from Marion Dougherty, the agent I'd signed with, telling me some movie producers were looking for a young Puerto Rican street-punk type for a leading role in a new movie. Was I interested? I'm not sure what my answer was, or if I gave her an answer, or even hung up the phone before I was out the door, down the stairs, and headed for the nearest subway to get to the audition.

I think, at that moment, if I had known exactly what I was letting myself in for; if I had known that for every Hollywood dream that comes true there's a heartbreak that goes with it or that, in a few short years, the life I had lived before that day would seem like it had belonged to someone else entirely; if I had been able to look into the future and see exactly what was in store—I don't think it would have changed my mind for a second. What I had been working toward for so long was suddenly within my reach, and I wasn't looking either backward or forward. My eyes were on the prize.

And, when I remember that time, I see that phone call as a decisive moment in setting the course of my life. Not long before, I had tried out for a part in a Lincoln Center Repertory Company production of *Camino Real* and was told not long after Marion's call that the producers had liked what they'd seen and were ready to offer me the role. I chose not to take the role, but to tell you the truth, it wasn't a difficult choice. I wanted to be in movies, to see myself on the big screen. That was where I was heading.

The movie part I was to try out for was playing Nicky Cruz, a real-life warlord of a fifties-era New York Puerto Rican gang, The Mau Maus. His story had been told in the best-selling book *The*

Cross and the Switchblade, written by the famous Christian evangelist David Wilkerson.

As told in the pages of *The Cross and the Switchblade*, Wilkerson had come to Spanish Harlem from his hometown of Phillipsberg, Pennsylvania, answering the call of God to preach the Gospel to the street gangs of New York. The toughest gang of that time was The Mau Maus, whose motto, tattooed on the arms of its members, was "Draw Blood."

Wilkerson's account of how he brought Nicky Cruz to Jesus made for some very compelling reading and it was only natural that Hollywood would sooner or later pick up on this inspiring, true-life saga. Don Murray was hired to direct the film because he had also co-produced and cowritten *The Hoodlum Priest*, which had similar subject matter.

Pat Boone played the preacher, but the heart of *The Cross and the Switchblade* was really in the story of Nicky Cruz, and for that vital role the producers were looking for a fresh young face.

Well I was young and my face was as fresh as my attitude; the only thing I had to do was convince them of what I already knew: I was Nicky Cruz. After all, hadn't Marion told me they were looking for a Puerto Rican actor who knew about street gangs and life in the projects? They might as well have written the part especially for me.

Of course, the casting directors didn't quite see it that way. At least not at first. After the initial audition I was called back five more times and each time I felt myself inching closer to locking in the part. But something seemed to be holding Don Murray back. Whatever it was, I was determined to win what I was convinced was mine.

I wasn't above asking for a little help. After every audition I headed right over to the church of St. Paul the Apostle, knelt down in a pew, and prayed like my life depended on it. "I just auditioned,

God," I told Him. "I think I was pretty good. They told me to come back. God, if I get this movie, I swear to you I'll get married in the church. You've got my word on it. So . . . how 'bout it?"

The auditions were all improvisations, held in a drafty downtown studio loft with risers at one end. Each time I came in they gave me a different situation to make up a scene about. I never quite knew what they were going to throw at me, but on my sixth go-round I came up with a scheme to turn the situation to my advantage. Stopping off at Forty-second Street, I ducked into one of those sleazy souvenir shops and actually bought a switchblade. After all, the movie was called *The Cross and the Switchblade*. I wanted to be the switchblade. It only seemed logical to "get in touch" with my character.

I tucked my new prop into my back pocket as I arrived at the audition, and listened dutifully to my improv instructions from the director.

"Okay, Hank," Murray told me, "here's the situation: You're in your gang clubhouse, minding your own business, and this preacher comes in, trying to mess with your head. He's talking about God and brotherly love and a better way to live and you're getting mad because you like your life just fine."

"Gotcha, Mr. Murray," I said and hopped up onto the stage. To set the mood, some extras were positioned around a table, so I walked up, leaned over, and kissed a girl playing one of the Mau Mau molls. Right around then, Pat Boone walked onto the stage, carrying a Bible.

"What the hell are you doin' here?" I said with a sneer.

He smiled serenely, showing off his perfect set of teeth. "Jesus loves you," Pat answered in his best preacher voice.

At that point I just let myself go, taking on the role of the short-fused hood like I was born for it. I grabbed Pat around the throat and shoved him against the wall. "You stay away from me," I snarled. "You stay away from my clubhouse. You stay away from my gang."

I was inches away from Pat's face, and although I could see that he was startled by my extreme form of method acting, he was professional enough to go along with the building emotions. "Jesus loves you," he croaked again.

It was then that I whipped the switchblade out of my pocket, flicked it open, and stuck the tip of the blade into one of his nostrils. "What did you say, preacher?" I demanded. Pat had gone from bright pink to ghostly pale. I held the pose for a few long beats before breaking character and turning to the director. "Like that, Mr. Murray?" I asked innocently.

I got the part there and then.

The first person I wanted to break the good news to was my mother. She didn't seem terribly impressed, at least not until I told her that I was going to get paid five hundred dollars a week for eight weeks. All of a sudden, this crazy dream her son had decided to chase wasn't so crazy. And even if it was, it was going to be one great-paying dream.

Those eight weeks of filming seemed both to fly by in eight minutes and to drag on for eight years. The days of a film shoot are typically long stretches of tedium interrupted by short frantic bursts of activity, which makes it both the longest and shortest way to pass the time that I know of.

Of course, I had already logged a lot of hours as an extra. As a lead actor though, I became isolated from the hands-on routines that occupy the lighting technicians, soundmen, teamsters, and all the other essential craftsmen without whom nothing would ever get on film. They were the people I liked the best on a film set, the working stiffs who made it happen behind the scenes, day in and day out. It was the kind of job full of camaraderie I could relate to, not so different, really, from working in a Laundromat or waiting tables.

As a "star," on the other hand, I was treated differently, and while *The Cross and the Switchblade* wasn't exactly a big-budget extravaganza, I knew that there were a lot of people looking to me to do good work. Their reputations and livelihood depended on making a movie come alive and I didn't take that responsibility lightly.

Between takes, I had time to develop a friendship with Pat Boone, a sweet, genuine man with a strong faith in God. At the same time, I was also working on a major crush on my leading lady Jackie Giroux. We were a hot and heavy item on the set, and the fact that she was going through a divorce at the time made it easier to pretend that there was more than there really was. But eventually I got the message that those on-camera kisses we rehearsed, and those cozy nights back at the hotel, were as fake as the switchblades the prop department supplied for the rumble scenes.

I also remember the day I actually met the man I portrayed. Nicky Cruz had taken his conversion seriously and become a minister in North Carolina. If you rent *The Cross and the Switchblade* today you can see him at the end of the movie delivering a personal message to the audience, which I still find very moving.

Although *The Cross and the Switchblade* was not produced or distributed by a major studio, word of the film's powerful message spread and it had a respectable box-office showing for a film with limited promotion. The movie really came into its own a few years after its release, when it became an important evangelism tool in prison ministries. Even though I might not have totally bought its Bible-thumping message, to this day I'm proud of the work I did in that film and of the effect it has had.

The real work on *The Cross and the Switchblade*, however, started after the wrap party. We were whisked off on a modest promotional tour, which took me to Hollywood for the first time, to appear at the movie's premiere. Hollywood, California, was a long way from the mean streets of Amsterdam Avenue, and the first extended trip I'd taken outside of that childhood summer in Puerto Rico. I tried to visit as many of the sights as I could. I even stopped by Mann's Chinese Theatre to try out my shoe size in the cement and visited John Garfield's star on Hollywood Boulevard.

Our next stop was Hawaii. The islands have had a special place in my heart ever since, combining those fond childhood memories of Puerto Rico's tropical paradise with a serenity and graciousness I've found nowhere else in the world.

Then, as quickly as it had begun, it was over. It's a hard fact of the entertainment industry that while it may take years to get a film made, the finished product will be in and out of the public's attention span in a matter of weeks or, at the most, months. More than a case of easy come, easy go, making movies is more like hard to come and easy to go, which is one reason not too many people have the temperament to stick it out in Hollywood.

As far as I was concerned, it had been too hard to get a real acting part to let anything go that easily. Once the production, premiere, and promotional tour were over, I got right back down to business, looking for the next starring vehicle.

My time in Hollywood convinced me that I needed to be where the action was. Besides, there was something about the balmy climate, the gently swaying palms, and the fast-lane lifestyle that made me want to stick around for a while. I had met a girl named Rosemary who worked at Empire Productions, the company that made *The Cross and the Switchblade*, and she offered to let me stay in her bungalow down a sunny side street in Beechwood Canyon, while I tried to turn up a new gig.

So, for the next six months I pounded the pavement like every other aspiring actor in Hollywood, sending out my publicity shot and résumé, and talking to agents, producers, and casting agents. I actually landed a brief representation contract with an independent agency, Jack Fields and Associates, but as far as plum roles dropping into my lap . . . well, let's just say the pickings were slim to none.

Since I had sent most of my paycheck back home, I was quickly running out of money at just about the same time Rosemary was getting tired of feeding me. I might have been stubborn, but I wasn't stupid. It was time to go back home and think through my options.

As it turned out, there weren't all that many options to choose from. Low on funds and without a real job, I was forced to move back in with my mom. Shortly after that, I picked up another weekend job on the recommendation of my old boss at Yellowfingers, waiting tables at another place he owned called Sign of the Dove at Sixty-fifth Street and Third Avenue.

And for the next two years it was once again business-as-usual. Did I feel discouraged or disillusioned at ending up back where I started after being in *The Cross and the Switchblade*? Did I think maybe Mom was right after all and that what I needed was a real job in the real world? Did I, in two whole years, lose faith in myself or my ability to act? The answer is no, no, and no.

Let's face it. I was young and full of hope and I had all the time in the world to get where I wanted to go. Now, a little older, certainly wiser and maybe sadder, I don't know if I could believe in myself that blindly ever again. But isn't taking chances and never thinking about tomorrow what being young is all about?

I utilized that long stretch of inactivity after *The Cross and the Switchblade* as well as I could, still scanning the trades to find occasional extra work and taking acting lessons with the legendary Mervin Nelson, whom I'd worked with earlier in my career in his upstairs studio at Fifty-fourth Street and Ninth Avenue. While there I learned that while I really wasn't much of a singer, I could carry a song just as well as anyone, by projecting a character. I polished my vocal, dancing, and dramatic chops under Mervin's intense and experienced eye. I felt that I was coming into my own, mastering the technical aspects of my craft. Mervin's manner of instruction was simple and direct. He tried to get all his students to bring something of themselves to the roles they played, and that was an approach that I understood, and responded to, instinctively.

Mervin was also the one who had helped me make one of the most important decisions any actor can make in his career. Back before I landed my role in *The Cross and the Switchblade*, I'd been dissatisfied with my given name. Henry Estrada just didn't have the right ring to it. Since most of the work that was coming my way was thanks to my Latin looks, it seemed only logical to try to cap-italize on that identity, so for a time I was calling myself Enrique Estrada. I even had publicity shots done up with that name.

When I consulted Mervin, however, he had different ideas. "En-rique Estrada," he said, letting the name, with all its Spanish *r*'s, roll off his tongue. "That's really going to typecast you, Hank."

I could see his point. While I certainly didn't mind getting work based solely on my ethnic heritage, when Mervin warned me how limited my acting range might become as a result, I knew he was right. But if I wasn't Hank, and I wasn't Enrique, who was I?

"I like what you're getting at with Enrique Estrada," Mervin con-tinued, thinking out loud. "It's got a nice sound to it. You just need to come up with something a little less like Ricky Ricardo."

"I've always liked Eric," I mused, for some reason thinking back on my old hippie girlfriend Erica.

"That's great!" was Mervin's enthusiastic response. "It's Latin, it's Scandinavian . . . it's catchy. But there's something missing. . . ." and I could see his wheels start to turn again. "How about Eric with a *k*?"

"Erik Estrada . . ." I tried it out a few times and, to be honest, I wasn't all that comfortable with my new identity. It wasn't just that

I'd never known a Puerto Rican kid named Eric, much less Erik. It just seemed like the name belonged to someone else, someone who had lived a completely different life from mine. But when I ran it by the rest of the actors in the studio, the response was pretty much the same as Mervin's had been. People liked it, liked the sound of it and the way it looked written on a piece of paper. I decided to go for it, and if I didn't exactly feel like me, maybe I'd grow into whoever I was supposed to be.

Even more important than Mervin's teaching skills and career advice was his encouragement. He always told me I had the talent to make something of myself and was consistently urging me to aim high and reach for the best I had inside me.

Aiming high was all well and good, but in the meantime I had to make money to supplement my meager income, so I started taking work as a photography model, appearing in various newspaper and magazine ads. It wasn't work I was exactly thrilled to do. How much acting is there in posing and looking pretty? But the pay was decent and it wasn't as if I was looking at an appointment book full of power lunches.

Actually, there was one modeling job that I did enjoy, involving a big mural being painted in the tearoom of the lobby of the Pierre Hotel. The mural is there to this day and if you happen to be in New York City, drop by. . . . I'm the dark-skinned guy with long hair.

The monotony of those long months was briefly broken when I finally got another acting job as part of an ensemble in a strictly B-grade prison drama called *Parades* (later retitled *The Line*). I was cast as—surprise—a smoldering Latino con. I got seven weeks' shooting in Florida out of the deal. But when it was all over, while I may have looked rested and even more tanned than usual, my career still hadn't budged an inch.

Chapter Seven

One of the most frustrating aspects of the career I chose is the inability of any actor to create work for himself. A songwriter can always write a tune, a painter can always fill a canvas, even if they're not getting paid a dime for their efforts. But unless you want to stand on a street corner in Times Square and do the monologue from Hamlet for passersby, it's almost impossible for an actor to create the opportunities to act.

The reason is that on both stage and screen, acting is part of a much larger artistic effort that involves the cooperation of dozens, or even hundreds, of other people. When the curtain goes up or the camera goes on, you may be the only focus of attention, but there's always going to be a whole team of people behind the scenes, making you look good. And until you can get onto that team, you might be the greatest actor since Olivier, but the only person who's going to know it will the one staring back at you in your bedroom mirror.

It's just the nature of the game: You wait and wait and then, if you're lucky, you get an audition and then you wait some more with your fingers numb from being crossed and your knees raw from praying. And all the time you're waiting and hoping and praying, you know in the back of your mind that your chances of actually getting the part have less to do with your skill as an actor or your suitability to the part than they do with whether the casting director got laid the night before or whether you remind him of the bully who used to beat him up on the playground.

People ask me all the time for helpful hints to break into acting as a career. I tell them that the first quality you've got to cultivate isn't empathy or passion or charisma, it's a hide as thick as a rhinoceros. That's the only way you'll be able to survive the disappointment, disillusionment, and just plain dumb luck that can either work for you or against you.

I have no idea whether all those would-be actors who approach me ever take that advice and learn to toughen up for the roller-coaster ride ahead, but I suspect that even if they do, it's never enough to prepare them. I can't say that I blame them for doubting how tough it's going to be, because I remember exactly how I felt as my acting life bumped and bounded down the runway, trying to get airborne.

Nothing was going to turn me, shake my confidence, or take the wind out from under my wings. Maybe I couldn't make them give me a part, but I could sure try. If sheer chutzpah was going to make the difference; if getting in their face and staying there would turn the tide; if being charming, outrageous, ingratiating, or just a simple pain in the ass would get their attention—then that's exactly what I was determined to do. It was like being a kid and getting double-dared to do something crazy. Just stand back and watch me. That was my attitude.

And after two years of waiting for my next break, you better believe I wore that attitude like an oversized chip on my shoulder. I wasn't just ready to prove myself; it was a matter of life or death. In other words, I was going to get another part or else . . .

*   *   *

Two years after my work on *The Cross and the Switchblade*, my first agent, Marion Dougherty, moved from the agency that had signed me, Kahn, Lifflander & Rhodes, to become an independent. I was now represented by one of the big guys, Jerry Kahn, and I guess he must have gotten tired of hearing my voice on the phone three times a day because when a part came up for a hot-tempered Latino, he knew just whom to call.

The movie being cast was an adaptation of the Joseph Wambaugh best-seller *The New Centurions*, a gritty police drama that had brought a whole new realism to the crime-story genre. I showed up early for my audition with the director, Richard Fleischer, with the lines for my tryout memorized down to the last comma. If landing this part had anything at all to do with my acting abilities, I was determined to give them the performance of a lifetime.

I'm not sure if I quite measured up to my own mental billing, but I did well enough to earn an appreciative nod from Fleischer. "I'd like you to come back tomorrow," he said. "The producers are flying in then and I'd like them to have a look at you." At that moment, it was like hearing the voice of God giving me the keys to the kingdom.

I practically camped out on the steps of the rehearsal loft where the auditions were taking place and was in top form the next morning when I tried out in front of the A-list producing team of Chartoff and Winkler, two of the most experienced and respected moviemakers in the business. It was an even more solid showing than my first time, and as I watched them huddle together in a whispered conference, I felt sure I had clinched the part.

"That was terrific, Erik," Fleischer said. "We'll be in touch."

It felt like I floated out of that studio and down the street. For the next few days, nothing could knock me off cloud nine. I was sure that any minute the phone would ring with the news that I should pack up, pick up my tickets, and get ready for my rendezvous with destiny in Hollywood.

Well, those minutes turned into hours, hours into days, and days into weeks. Two weeks, exactly, before I called my agent to find out what the hell had happened to my sure thing.

That was when I was told that the whole casting office had moved back to Hollywood without a word to all the actors who'd been left hanging after their auditions. It was typical Hollywood behavior, but I didn't let that stop me.

"Is the part still open?" I asked Jerry, and he put me on hold for a few endless minutes while he checked.

"It's still open" were his words when he came back on the line. "They haven't cast it yet."

"Look," I said, with what I guess must have been a keen edge of determination, or maybe desperation, in my voice. "If I go out to California, can you get me in for another audition?"

"Well," Jerry replied, "if they'd really wanted you, Erik, I'm sure—"

"Just tell me—" I interrupted. "Can you get me in? Yes or no?"

"I'll try," he said.

That was all I needed. I collected that week's paycheck from work and, borrowing a few more dollars from my mother, caught the first flight to the coast.

It was the first time I'd been in Hollywood since shooting *The Cross and the Switchblade*. I got a room at the Roosevelt Hotel, right across the street from Mann's Chinese Theatre, and perched myself next to the phone, calling Jerry at what must have been half-hour intervals. My window of opportunity was small and getting smaller all the time. I had enough money to last three days and not a penny more. If I didn't get the job by then, I'd be hitchhiking back to Amsterdam Avenue.

Finally, on the morning of the third day, I got the call I'd been waiting for. If I hurried down to the production office, I could just maybe have a shot at getting seen again. The appointment was tentative, depending on how busy Fleischer and the producers were, and Jerry wasn't making any promises. If this was going to happen at all, I was going to have to make it happen.

As I took the bus uptown to Columbia Studios, where preproduction work on *The New Centurions* was starting to kick into high gear, I weighed my options. This was no time to be polite, stand on ceremony, or wait around the lobby, hoping to get noticed. By the time those bus doors hissed open at my stop, I'd worked up a real head of steam and let it carry me past the gates and right into the bungalow offices of Chartoff and Winkler. I didn't even stop at the secretary's desk but headed straight for the inner sanctum with her shouting for security as she trailed behind me.

As soon as I burst into the room I realized that whatever Jerry had told them, they certainly were not expecting me to barge in at that particular moment. In fact, the look of shock on their faces led me to believe they weren't expecting me at all. The last place they'd laid eyes on me was three thousand miles away. Since that time they had auditioned dozens of other young actors for the role that I was determined to make mine.

It was just that element of complete surprise that I used to my advantage. "Hello, Mr. Fleischer," I said with my broadest, whitest smile. "Hello, Mr. Chartoff and Mr. Winkler. I'm sure there must have been some mistake back in New York about the role I auditioned for. You left without telling me whether I had it or not."

"Well," said Chartoff, still trying to recover from my grand entrance. "We weren't exactly sure—"

"That's just what I thought," I said without letting him finish. "You wanted to try out a few more people. I can certainly understand that. With a big production like this you've got to be absolutely sure." I moved across the room and stood right in front of the table where all three were sitting. "And now that you've seen all the others, I'd like to give you a chance to see me again." Without waiting for them to say a word, I stepped back and began my scene, one in which my character, a young rookie cop, really starts to crack under the strain of the job. If I do say so myself, it was dynamite.

I guess they thought so, too. They gave me the part right on the spot.

Landing that role in *The New Centurions* felt like winning the Triple Crown, the Heavyweight Championship, and the World Series all wrapped into one. It was a starring role in a major motion picture, with a budget that was easily ten times bigger than *The Cross and the Switchblade*. For the first time I would have the benefit of some real movie muscle behind me. The studio promotion machine would be cranking out my name and face across the country and around the world. I'd be seeing myself on a giant poster in Times Square and in the guest chair on *The Tonight Show*. Old friends would talk about knowing me way back when and new friends would be crowding around me, just wanting to bask in the glow of genuine stardom.

In short, my head started swelling dangerously. Wasn't this proof that I was every inch the actor, the raw material of the legend that I'd always been in my own private fantasies? It had taken the rest of the world a long time to catch up, but now they knew what I knew: Erik Estrada was hot.

But not, as it turned out, all that hot. The first pinprick that punctured my balloon came when I discovered that for the role of the seasoned veteran cop in *The New Centurions*, the producers were actively negotiating with none other than George C. Scott. Scott had just come off the biggest movie of the year, *Patton*, which had earned him a Best Actor Oscar. Well, as soon as he agreed to take the part, the whole focus of the movie underwent a radical change.

Before that, the heart of the story had been my character, that hot-blooded young rookie who takes on more than he can handle and ends up committing suicide. But when George C. Scott took what had been a secondary role, the script immediately went back to the writers for some major revisions. Now it was my role that took a backseat to Scott's character, and instead of starring in *The New Centurions*, I was co-starring with an actor who could really draw at the box office.

Actually, by the time we actually started shooting, the story had undergone a total transformation, becoming much more of an ensemble piece than originally written, which meant I was suddenly sharing billing not only with an Oscar winner but with other up-and-coming actors like Stacy Keach, Scott Wilson, and Rosalind Cash.

Okay, I told myself, so *The New Centurions* wasn't exactly going to be my ticket to the top. I was quickly learning that surviving in Hollywood was all about rolling with the punches and I could roll with the best of them. Besides, there were some very definite compensations for losing top billing to George C. Scott.

First on the list was just the chance to be back in Tinseltown again. Returning to New York after *The Cross and the Switchblade* may have been financially necessary, but I'd always had the feeling that being away from the center of the action had really set my career back. Second was the thousand dollars a week I'd be getting for eight weeks' work, which sounded like a not-so-small fortune.

Finally, what I suppose turned out to be the most valuable asset of all, was the chance to work up close with an actor of the caliber of Scott. A gentleman, a true professional, and, most important, a man who knew what it was like to struggle for a chance to work and work hard to keep that chance alive, George was a pure joy to be around. He never hogged the scenes we shared and never seemed to take his star status all that seriously. To him, the absurdities of Hollywood, the ability you had to have to cultivate politics and personal charm, had not only toughened his hide but given him a keen sense of humor. He offered me some of the best advice I ever got in show business. He told me not to take myself too seriously, and never, ever, believe my own hype. To him, the movie business was a big game, and his was an attitude that, while I didn't exactly share it, I could certainly appreciate.

Shooting a movie is, in many ways, a true test of character. The pressure can easily overwhelm an inexperienced actor. At the same time it can turn a star into a selfish child. At its best, shooting a movie fosters the kind of camaraderie that soldiers in the same squad share. It's a brief but intense connection that can either leave you friends for life or hating each other. During *The New Centurions*, I made a lot of friends.

Some of those friends weren't even in the movie business. For my two-month stay in Hollywood I needed a place to stay and a way to get to and from the studio. I found a one-bedroom apartment in Burbank and, as soon as I was settled in, dropped by Enterprise Rent-a-Car to get a set of wheels.

The guy who owned the lot was named Irv Fox. He not only rented me a big old Cadillac at a bargain price, but even invited me over to his house for a meal. There I met his wife, Sheila, and his three little kids, all of whom treated me like a member of the family. Although I lived in that cracker-box apartment off Burbank Boulevard, I found a home away from home with the Foxes.

My friendship with that family has stood the test of time, unlike those fleeting feelings I had after *The New Centurions* finished the last day of shooting and we drained the last bottle of champagne at the wrap party. In retrospect, I guess I should have learned my lesson from *The Cross and the Switchblade*—that much of the excitement and attention generated by a movie burns off as quickly as fog under the hot Los Angeles sun. The myth in Hollywood has always been that you're only as good as your last role. But I've learned a different rule to live by: You're only as good as your upcoming role.

People in the movie business, where cutthroat competition is the name of the game, are always waiting for the guys on top to take a fall. There's something sick in the way they gleefully anticipate the failure of others. All of which means that as long as you've got another project waiting in the wings—as long as you're not a has-been, an also-ran, or a wannabe—they've got to give you respect, because no one knows whom they might be working with, or for, tomorrow. The only people they can afford to kick around are the ones who've bombed at the box office, lost a bidding war for some hot new script, or not found something new to do fifteen minutes after their last movie wrapped.

Contrary to popular belief, success in Hollywood doesn't necessarily breed more success. Each time out, you've got to prove yourself all over again, and one bad role, one miscast part or career misstep, and you're back to square one. Those are the rules of the game. If you don't like it, there's always someone else in the wings, waiting to take your place.

While *The New Centurions* didn't exactly knock them into the aisles, it did a respectable business and reflected well, I think, on my abilities as a screen actor. My role may have been small in the end, but I did the best with what I had and turned in a credible performance.

From my mom's point of view, my career was a whole lot more than credible. As far as she was concerned, I had arrived. When I got back to New York, I took her out to see *The New Centurions* at a theater on Broadway. Right across the street, another theater was showing *The Cross and the Switchblade* at the bottom half of some bargain double bill.

So there I was, with my name on marquees on both sides of the street and it did my heart good to see how proud that sight made my mother. Despite her initial misgivings, she had come around to support and encourage me when she saw how serious I was about acting, and her approval had made all the difference in the tough times. As much as I wanted to succeed to prove myself, I also wanted to make her proud. That day on Broadway, that's exactly what I had done. That was the kind of success I could really take to the bank.

Which was lucky, because I wasn't taking too much else to the bank at that time. The pattern that had been set with *The Cross and the Switchblade* repeated itself with *The New Centurions*. I returned to New York, expecting a hero's welcome, and all I found was my old apron waiting at the restaurant and my old room in the Amsterdam projects, looking smaller and more forlorn than ever. After everything I'd done, I was back where I'd started and that slow slide into dull reality was definitely getting old.

This time, however, I was determined that if circumstances weren't going to change for me, I would make some changes on my own. With the money I'd socked away from *The New Centurions*, I finally had the ability to get my mother out of the crumbling projects apartment we'd called home for so long. I had my sister, Carmen, do a little real estate hunting and she found a nice, spacious new apartment out in Rego Park in Queens. It was there that I set my mother up in high style and listened with pleasure as she bragged about me to her new neighbors.

It was a whole new world for her and a great way to underscore the fact that for all the trouble she'd had early in her life, things had turned out not so bad after all. In fact, our immediate family was flourishing. Carmen had gotten married to a nice guy named Myron and had a good-paying job as a secretary, while Joey, my foster brother, had become a photographer, working in a portrait studio. He was living in his own place, a walk-up just above Joe Allen, and I'd often stay there when I was working or after a long day of auditions.

I was going out for anything and everything I could find, including modeling work and bit parts on daytime dramas. I had promised

My sister, Carmen, and I, circa 1952

My sister, Carmen, my mother, and I, age eight, dressed in our best for Carmen's confirmation

The Estrada
family when I
was ten

With my mother,
Carmen Estrada,
and my
grandmother,
Paguita Cardona,
in 1978, just
before I was to
lead the Puerto
Rican Day
Parade as grand
marshal

My first major role was in *The New Centurions* in 1971.

As Nicky Cruz in *The Cross and the Switchblade*

An early publicity photograph, 1973

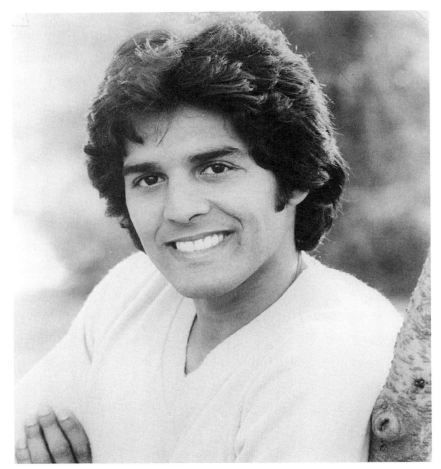

With my best friend, Don't Cry, in 1978

"Ponch"

This was one of my best-selling posters, 1980.

Larry Wilcox and I in the California Highway Patrol uniforms that made us
so famous *CHiPs*, copyright © 1977 by Turner Entertainment Co. All rights reserved.

With my mom when my arm was in a cast, shortly after my motorcycle accident

myself that I would read the trade magazines every day and drop off my photo and résumé somewhere at least once a week. At the same time, I went back to Mervin Nelson's studio to continue my acting classes.

Once I settled in again, I realized for a fact that New York just wasn't the place to nurture a movie career. It was right about that time that I got another call from my agent, this time asking me if I wanted to do a guest spot on the hot new television show *Hawaii Five-O*. I jumped at the chance, of course, not only because it was a plum role, playing the ruthless son of the character played by Simon Oakland, but also because I'd have an opportunity to revisit Hawaii. The islands were everything I remembered and the shoot ended all too quickly. Almost before I knew it, I was back home, wondering, one more time, what had hit me.

There was one moment that stands out over all the others as a mark of how frustrated I was with the on-again, off-again pace of my career. I had been invited by some friends at Mervin's studio to go to a party, and since they were a pretty lively bunch to begin with, I knew it would be a lot of fun. But something held me back and, making up some lame excuse, I begged off.

Later, sitting alone in Joey's apartment, I turned over the incident in my mind. What had made me decline the invitation? The harder I thought about it, the clearer it became. I could see myself in the happy crowd, maybe talking to some good-looking girl, and she would invariably ask me what I did for a living. "I'm an actor," I'd say and then, of course, she would ask what I'd been in and what I was doing now. And I'd have to explain that, while I'd had a couple of co-starring roles in major motion pictures, right at the moment I was waiting tables and sleeping on the sofa at my brother's apartment. It was a scene I just didn't want to subject myself to. The next time I go to a party, I promised myself, people are going to know who I am, and what I'm doing.

But until that time came, I had to deal with the fact that, for all my pushy, cocky, self-confident attitude, I was still just another out-of-work actor pounding the pavement. I needed a real change, a fresh start, a new beginning.

And when I got it, I grabbed it with both hands. I was told that *Hawaii Five-O* needed me to fly out to the Coast to do some looping for my episode, which meant that I had to re-record some of the dialogue that hadn't come out clearly on location because of the background noise. A few days later, a first-class ticket was delivered to my mother's apartment.

I held that ticket in my hands, turning it over as my thoughts turned over in my head. It was right about then that my mother walked into the room.

"Mom," I said, "I have to go to California to do some more work."

"That's nice," she replied, only half listening as she flipped through the pages of a magazine.

"But, Mom," I persisted, and this time, at the tone in my voice, she looked up. "This time I'm gonna stay out there."

She sat down on the couch as if the weight of the world had just fallen on her shoulders. I crossed the room, the ticket still in my hand, and sat down next to her. "Are you gonna be all right, Mom?" I asked, looking into her eyes.

She stared back for a long moment, then sighed. "Papo," she said, "do you remember when you were just a little boy and I took you to see the Gypsy fortune-teller?"

I did. She had dragged me into a neighborhood storefront, decorated with palm-reading charts, pictures of the Virgin Mary and a collection of saints, and plastic palm fronds shading the windows. She paid to have some old woman with a scarf on her head and jangling gold bracelets on her wrists read my fortune. I didn't want anything to do with this old-country superstition, but she insisted, and like I've said, once my mother made up her mind, resistance was futile.

The fortune-teller laid her cards on the table while muttering some mystic incantation over them. Then she looked me straight in the eye like she could pierce right through to my very soul, and at that moment I felt a chill run up my spine.

"You will stand in front of many people," the old Gypsy intoned. "They will all be watching you and giving to you their love and respect."

I remembered the scene vividly the moment my mother reminded me. "She was just some old woman," I said, but my mother shook her head solemnly.

"No, Papo," she replied. "She knew. And when she told you what your future would be, with all the people watching you, I knew that I would not be able to hold you back." Tears filled her eyes. "So now, you go, Papo," she said. "Now you will get the love and respect of all the people."

I must have cried then too, because I remember seeing her face as if through a haze. I guess we hugged a long time, because I remember feeling her small body in my arms even after I'd gotten up to leave. I must have promised her that I'd be back to get her soon, because I remember her nodding and smiling as she dried her own tears.

But what I remember most is when she took the airplane ticket out of my hands and scanned it until she found the price. She shook her head, impressed. "First-class, all the way," she said.

"First class from now on, Mom," I answered.

"I tell you what, Papo," she continued, pressing the ticket back into my hand. "You take this first-class ticket. You trade it in and buy round-trip fare. Then you'll always have a way to come back to me."

And that's what I did. Because when my mother makes up her mind, that's all there is to it.

Chapter Eight

My move to California wasn't exactly the biggest news to hit the state in the early spring of 1971. What was grabbing the headlines at the time was the aftermath of the devastating Sylmar earthquake, which clocked in at almost seven points on the Richter scale and shook up a whole lot of people. I took it as an omen that I was going to rattle a few windows myself.

The ground was still trembling from aftershocks when I got off the plane in early March of that year and immediately started looking for a place to live. I found an apartment building in the San Fernando Valley called, appropriately enough, Club California.

The little studio space wasn't much to look at, but for me, it held a special charm. It was the first place I could truly call my own, a haven where I could leave my underwear on the floor if I wanted to, a home I didn't have to share with anyone. It was a good thing I didn't either, because I don't think I could have fit a another person in there. The refrigerator and two-burner stove took up about half the available space, and in the rest I crammed myself and my few belongings: a portable television and stereo, a single bed, and a few pictures for the nightstand. To liven things up I went down to Pier One Imports and bought some of those Indian tapestry bedspreads and tacked them to the ceiling, giving the place the feel of an Arab sheik's desert tent. By this time I hardly had enough room to turn around, so I went to the hardware store and bought enough mirrored stick-on squares to cover one whole wall. Now at least, I had the illusion of space. And wasn't illusion, I asked myself, the name of the game out here in Hollywood?

Rent on my new pad was one hundred and fifty dollars a month, which worked out to about five dollars a square foot, but I had access to the Club California Jacuzzi, pool, gym, and barbecue pit, along with my very own parking spot. What else could a young single guy possibly require?

Except, of course, something to put into that parking space. My next stop was to a used-car lot, where I bought the first car I could really call my own, a battered '67 Galaxy 500 with a shredded ragtop and a bottomless appetite for gas and oil to feed that mighty V-8. As far as I was concerned, it might just as well have been a Rolls. After all, it was all mine, bought and paid for, eight hundred dollars in cash.

By this time my bankroll was pretty well tapped out, so I started hunting around for a part-time job to keep body and soul together while I waited for the big break that was surely just around the corner. I stopped by to see Irv Fox. When I told him I was here to stay this time, the first thing he did was invite me over to his house for a big spaghetti dinner with the family.

That night, as the pasta bowl was passed around the table, I piled my plate so high that Irv's three-year-old daughter, Terry, pointed at me and piped up, "He took too much!" I guess at that point my need for a job must have been crystal clear because after dinner, Irv offered to let me work at his lot, washing and vacuuming cars after the customers turned them in. "It'll be perfect for you, Erik," he said. "If you get an audition you can just jump in one of the cars and take off. That way you won't be tied down in case something big comes up." I could have kissed him. Irv is, without a doubt, one of the sweetest and most giving people I've ever met and one more in a line of surrogate fathers that includes Papa Don Pino and Pete Panos.

Working for Irv at Enterprise was a sweet deal as long as my unemployment checks kept coming in to supplement my part-time pay, but once they ran out, I was forced to find a second job to make ends meet.

I landed one as a doorman, bouncer, and all-around trouble-shooter at a rough-and-tumble Harley bar called the Red Chariot, right on the main drag at the bad end of the Valley. I was working out pretty regularly at the time, pumping iron in the gym at Club California and running five miles a day around the track at North Hollywood High, so I was in pretty good shape to handle any problem. But I also did my best to bring an element of class to the joint, coming to work in a blazer and inviting any pretty girl I met around town to the bar for free drinks.

My partner in this improvement project was the Red Chariot's bartender, Vic McCain, a good-looking guy with blond hair and blue eyes who was also into bodybuilding. Between the two of us we pretty much covered the romantic bases—dark and light, Latin and all-American—and it wasn't long before we had stocked the place with great-looking women, which in turn brought a whole new clientele around. We were well on our way to turning the Red Chariot into the Valley's premier watering hole for singles.

At that time, however, I was a lot less interested in playing the field than I let on, because I was already seriously involved with someone. Her name was Robin Miller and she worked as a secretary for Berry Gordy, the founder and president of Motown Records. Motown's offices were right down the street from the Enterprise lot and we used to run into each other on the street or at the neighborhood lunch counter.

Robin was the kind of person whose natural goodness brimmed over in the warmth of her smile and the sparkle in her eyes. After our first few dates, she took me to meet her family. They were very respectable citizens who lived in an upscale neighborhood in Reseda and who didn't seem to care that I was basically an out-of-work actor from the projects, hustling for every dime. It was in line with a laid-back attitude I was discovering to be part of the California lifestyle. I'm not saying that race and class prejudices are any better in sunny Southern California than anywhere else. It just seemed to me that people were more willing to accept you for who you were instead of where you came from. Maybe that's because most people in L.A. come there from somewhere else, reinventing themselves in a place where no one looks back. I liked that about my new home, just like I liked the fact that Robin's father looked me right in the eyes when he shook my hand.

As those first months in Los Angeles settled into a routine of work and play, late nights and long weekends, I felt myself settle into a different rhythm of life. My ambition still burned bright, but I didn't have that restless urge always to be moving forward, like a shark that has to keep swimming to live. I could afford to take a little time to myself now, go out with Robin to the bar or to see *The Way We Were*, one of her favorite movies. It was a feeling that, sooner or later, things would fall my way, and if it wasn't today . . . well, there was always tomorrow.

I guess eventually I let things get a little too laid-back, because Robin started slipping away from me. I'm not sure whether she dated other guys as a way to force me to make a commitment, or whether she was just caught up in the live-and-let-live spirit that was so much a part of that sprawling city. But after discovering that she'd gone to a few parties without me, and after calling a few times from the bar on a Saturday night to find no one home, I decided that enough was enough. Robin was a beautiful girl with all kinds of guys interested in getting close to her. Since the last thing I wanted to do was settle down, it was only natural that she would start to drift away. But, natural or not, I nursed my broken heart for months afterward, as the first dark cloud of disappointment passed across the sunny paradise that had become my life.

There were, thankfully, compensations, and not just the all-too-willing girls I had lured into the Red Chariot. As my first year in L.A. drew to a close, I signed with a new agency and began regularly going up for auditions. They were mostly small parts in episodic TV, but at least I was getting seen and heard.

Not that it did much good, at least in the beginning. It seemed like every part I tried out for would go to someone else, and more often than not, the guy who landed the job looked a lot like me. The situation came to a head one day when I walked into a casting office at Universal Studios to audition for a small role in *The Six Million Dollar Man*. When I opened the door to the waiting room, twelve pairs of dark, Latin eyes turned to give me the once-over. Everyone in that room could have been my brother.

And it was at that moment that I finally figured it out. "They don't care about my acting," I said to myself as I took a seat at the end of the line. "All they're interested in is a look." Well, I was going to give them something else to get interested in. I was going to do that audition my way.

When my turn finally came around, I walked into an all-too-familiar setup, a bored-looking producer and director sitting behind a table, a pile of eight by tens and résumés in front of them, and a harried secretary taking notes on who was in and who wasn't.

I stood calmly in front of them and said, "Look. I know that you've seen twenty guys just like me today, and they've all read the same lines in the same way. I'm going to try to give you something a little different. But I have a tendency sometimes to go over the top with a part, so if I get too intense, just let me know."

They nodded and I could tell I'd gotten their attention. I launched into the part, that of a cheap Chicano hood, giving it everything I had and then some, shouting out my lines and throwing myself around like I was about to jump off the stage and attack them. I don't know whether I was any better than anyone else that day, but my guess is that my little warm-up speech had given me the edge I needed. I got the part.

From then on, my approach to auditions changed. I was no longer intimidated by a room full of Latin clones, no longer cowed by the thought of all that competition. I was through second-guessing myself and trying to read the minds of the people behind those desks. I knew I had the look; otherwise I wouldn't have been called. I also knew I had the acting chops. All I had to do was let myself go. It was an edge that started working for me consistently.

Of course, I wasn't leaving anything to chance, either. As soon as I got home from an audition I got down on my knees and prayed like a saint; then I called my mother and got her to pray for me, too. I had a feeling God would listen to her prayers before He'd get around to mine, but I think Mom wasn't always that sure herself. Two or three days after I made those calls, I'd always get a letter from her with ten or twenty bucks in it, just in case.

After that *Six Million Dollar Man* part, things really started to fall my way. I went up for a role in *Joe Forrester*, which starred Lloyd Bridges in a spin-off series from *Police Story*. Then, in quick succession, I landed parts on *Kojak*, *Owen Marshall*, *Mannix*, and a return engagement on *The Six Million Dollar Man*. I was always cast in more or less the same part, an intense, fiery-eyed Latin, and though the roles were pretty much interchangeable, I wasn't complaining. The steady work was something I needed for my wallet—and ego.

Between television gigs, I started landing small supporting roles in movies; first on a B-grade quickie called *Trackdown* and then as Julio, the romantic flight engineer, in *Airport 1975*.

The day I found out about getting the part in *Airport 1975*, I vividly remembered an incident that had happened to me when I was only sixteen. It had been around the time my mother started going to see the fortune-teller who predicted that I would one day stand before many admiring people. The Gypsy had a friend, a mysterious man from Cuba named Roger Fonseca, and a few days later I went with my aunt Lucy for a consultation with him at his apartment on Dyckman Street.

There was something about this character, a hidden wisdom and spirituality that drew me to him right away. He told me that before he would do a reading with me, I needed to take a bath scented with yellow roses, honey, cinnamon, and a teaspoon of sugar. The reason, he told me, was to "sweeten my vibes."

Part of me thought that Fonseca was just a crazy old coot, but there was another part that was intrigued by his charismatic personality and the aura of power that seemed to emanate from him. I did as I was instructed and only later did I find out the bath ritual dated back to African religions from before the time of Christ.

I would also later discover that Roger was not simply a storefront psychic but what would come to be known as a channeler, a man with the power to summon spirits from the other side.

And that's exactly what he did after I returned, smelling like some kind of a birthday-cake recipe. He had gathered several other people in his living room, and with his cigar and glass of rum by his side, he would call up an old Spanish spirit named Francisco.

It was spooky and hard to believe, but Roger had an authority about him that was difficult to deny. As I watched him fall into a trance and begin speaking in the soft voice of another spirit, I had no doubt that what I was experiencing was real.

Francisco spoke only Spanish but seemed to understand everything, even though we asked our questions in English. It wasn't very long into the session when Roger, under the influence of Francisco, turned to me and told me, in a clear and unwavering voice, that I was going to be successful in *la caja*.

I may not have known much Spanish but I knew that word—the box. "You mean television," I whispered and Roger/Francisco nodded, then continued speaking in Francisco's voice. "And you will also be in the movies," he said. "You will be on the silver screen and with you will be . . . Myrna Loy."

Myrna Loy? That was a little more than I could wrap my teenage mind around. But years later, when I was told whom was I was going to be working with in *Airport 1975*, the name Myrna Loy leaped out from all the others. Francisco had been right.

Roger Fonseca and I have kept in touch ever since that first night, and he, too, became a kind of surrogate father figure for me. I even came to call him by the name "Padrino," "Godfather," and to this day he is an honored guest in my house.

With my role in *Airport 1975*, I was finally able to quit working at the Red Chariot because what had started out as a three-day job at five hundred dollars a day turned into eight weeks at the same pay, as the production lagged behind schedule and went way over budget. It was a whole lot better than the fifteen dollars a night I was making as a bouncer, and besides, with my career finally beginning to click, I had a lot less free time on my hands. I also still had unemployment to fall back on, and at the end of every two-or three-day job I got, I'd reapply. Going to the unemployment office was a week-to-week routine that any experienced actor knows cold.

I was also beginning to move in a better circle of friends and associates. From those eight weeks on the set of *Airport 1975* I got close to the great comic actor Larry Storch, probably best known for his work in *F Troop*. Through Larry I met the actress Anna Navarro. She had a lot of contacts in the executive suites at Universal Studios, whose television division dominated episodic TV in the early seventies. Whenever I auditioned for a role, Anna was always the first call I made, after my mother. If the show was, for example, *McMillan and Wife*, she would invariably know the producer or director or executive in charge of production, and the good words she put in for me made a lot of difference.

Anna was Puerto Rican herself, and while we were never romantically involved, we developed a relationship that was as close as any brother and sister tie. As part of my regular workout routine, I'd stop by her house to pick up her dog Silly and take him running with me every morning.

I also got tight with a publicist named Ken Baxter, who had his own firm. Ken was also Puerto Rican (he changed his name for the business), and it was because of that cultural tie that he offered to do my publicity for free while I was getting started.

Ken and Anna, along with her son Tommy, his wife, Maria, and Anna's sister Goodie, have always loved and encouraged me. I'll always be grateful to them.

At that time there was an increasing awareness of the cultural diversity that existed in America. The entertainment business, always anxious to exploit new audiences, was actively seeking out Latin types to give their shows an up-to-date racial mix. Of course, stereotypes still abounded, and most of the roles I got picked for were variations on the Chicano criminal or innocent immigrant theme. It didn't matter if the part called for a Mexican peasant or an aristocratic Spanish lover. If you had the look, you were in and there was no doubt that I was on a major roll.

One of the biggest thrills for me was landing a guest starring role on *Baretta*. For me, Robert Blake had a hard edge and intense focus that I wanted to cultivate in my own work and he was one of the few actors that I really admired. I was a big fan of *Baretta* and would always set aside my Wednesday nights for a special ritual. After running my five miles, I would stop by the neighborhood Häagen-Dazs for a pint of chocolate chip, settle into my little bed, turn on my little TV, and watch my Wednesday night lineup straight through: *Sanford and Son* and *Baretta*, rounded off by a late show of *Dean Martin Presents*. That was my idea of an evening of quality viewing and you can imagine my delight when I was tapped for a big part in a *Baretta* episode.

The role I landed was what's called "top of the show," which basically means I was getting guest-star billing. The difference between that and a regular part was worked out in dollars and cents. For a regular appearance in an hour drama, which usually meant a three-day shoot, the going rate was one thousand dollars. The top of the show guest star made five hundred dollars a day, which right away meant that I was making half again as much money on a standard three-day shoot. If the schedule went over, you'd still be clocking the same amount, and it wasn't unusual for some of the shows to run into three or even four days of extra shooting.

But what interested me far more than the money was a shot at working with Robert Blake. The episode I'd signed on for had me in the role of an undercover cop, put in prison on an investigation with Detective Baretta. I worked my tail off to get the part down right, practicing my lines over and over in front of a mirror, trying my best to get down everything from attitude to accent. I even went to the trouble of dirtying up my teeth to get that jailhouse look and generally made myself as scuzzy as possible.

Well, the show turned out successfully and Blake let it be known that he was impressed with my work. So impressed, in fact, that a few days after we wrapped, he called my agency with an intriguing offer. He wanted me to be a regular for the remainder of *Baretta*'s current season, thirteen shows at one thousand dollars a week.

It didn't take a rocket scientist to see that a great opportunity was staring me in the face. On the other hand, it also didn't take a lot to figure out that Blake was trying to low-ball me on the price he'd pay. If I was going to be getting top of the show billing as a regular, the price should have been more in the neighborhood of $4,500 weekly. Was Robert Blake playing me for a chump?

I asked the advice of my agent at Fields and Associates, a young go-getter named Mark Harris. "It's up to you," he said. "We've been building your career steadily and there's no reason to believe that things won't continue this way. Of course, getting a regular spot on a top-rated show like *Baretta* is a tempting offer, but you've got to ask yourself if you couldn't be making more money, and getting just as much exposure, doing what you're doing now."

It was a good point, but I was still unsure. There were so many angles to take into consideration: Was I being low-balled because I was Puerto Rican? Was the chance to work with someone I admired as much as Blake worth taking a cut in pay? Was my drive to be a star more powerful than my drive for financial security?

The only way I could figure out how to make this decision was to talk to Blake himself, so I made an appointment to come by and see him one day in his trailer on the set.

I was a little nervous going in, I'll admit, but this was business and I was sure that between two fellow actors we could work it out.

Blake, dressed in his trademark black T-shirt, greeted me warmly, shaking my hand and offering me a seat. "Did you get my offer?" he asked, right up front.

"Mr. Blake," I said as respectfully as I knew how, "I want to tell you, first of all, how much I admire you as an actor and for what you've accomplished on this show. I think your character is one of the most real and believable ones on TV and I don't miss a single night if I can help it." He must have seen what was coming, because his face suddenly got all hard and squint-eyed, but I took a deep breath and kept on going. "I appreciate the offer you've made to me, but the salary you've offered isn't as much as I might have hoped. I've been building my career step by step for some time now and I think I've gotten to the point where . . . well, let's just say I'm worth more than that."

A long pause followed. Blake stared at me as if I were a cockroach that had crawled onto his dinner. He stood up, knocking his chair over, and really let me have it, both barrels. "You know what, kid?" he shouted. "You're a real asshole. And your agents are real assholes. Let me tell you something, smartass. Ten years from now I'm still gonna be here, on top, and ten years from now, you're still gonna be running around looking for it. Now get the hell out of here."

I stood up and in that split second considered flooring the arrogant bastard. But something stopped me. More than anger, I realized that what I was feeling was sadness. Here was a guy I had looked up to, even idolized, somebody I wanted to model my own career after. And when it came right down to it, he was as phony and full of himself as all the other inflated egos floating around Hollywood like hot-air balloons. I was mad at him for being so cheap and mean, and I was mad at myself for falling for his whole fake facade of the streetwise, blue-collar guy.

So instead of getting right back in his face, I just turned and walked away, out of that trailer and off the lot without looking back. That sense of sadness, of being cheated (even though I hadn't taken his offer), stayed with me for weeks. Is that what acting was all about? Is that what happened to people when they got to the top? If it was, I didn't want any part of it. But at the same time, I sure didn't want to get off the train just as it was finally pulling out of the station.

It was then that I made another promise to myself, as solemn and sincere as the one I'd made in Herald Square to always have money in my pocket. "I'm never going to get fooled by appearances again," I told myself. "And if I ever get to the top, I'm not going to forget where I came from."

It was a promise that was about to be put to the test.

Chapter Nine

Three years after my arrival in Hollywood I felt as if I had actually created my own eight-pointer on the show-business Richter scale. One guest-starring role led to another, and by 1975, there was hardly a time when my name didn't appear more than once in the program listing for any given edition of *TV Guide*.

I was appearing with increasing frequency on every major hour-long drama regardless of the studio or network, one show coming right on top of another. From a job on *McMillan and Wife* I picked up a role on Angie Dickenson's red-hot cop show *Police Woman*. And if Robert Blake had showed me the ugly side of being a star, Angie demonstrated all that was graceful and generous and giving about the profession. Her way of treating everyone on the set with respect, from co-stars to gofers, set an example that I've tried to follow ever since.

Movie roles kept pace with my television work, and while the jobs I got might not have had the same impact on audiences, I made sure to consider seriously every film offer that came my way. My eyes, in short, were still on that particular prize of a career in film. I got a small but meaty role in the World War II drama *Midway*, thanks to director Jack Smight, who had hired me for *Airport 1975* and liked my work enough to cast me again. I also landed a supporting part in an Irwin Allen disaster extravaganza called *Fire!*, in which I played against Patty Duke, Ernest Borgnine, and Alex Cord.

But for the most part, the emphasis was on television, and I was more than willing to go with the flow. By this time I had gotten rid of that smoking old Galaxy, selling it as parts for $150 and bought myself a nice Mercedes coupe, for $2,500 cash. I'd also moved out of my little mirrored closet and into a more spacious one-bedroom apartment not far away in Studio City. The place had a sweeping, third-floor view of the Hollywood Hills. On more than one night I would stare up at the twinkling lights of those mansions on the hill and vow that one day I'd be up there too, looking down on the Valley and remembering the life I used to live.

As the new television season approached, there was the same sudden flurry of activity that greeted every new year. Shows that were dropping in the ratings were yanked and a whole new crop of dramas and sitcoms jostled for one of the few open slots on the network schedules. It's called pilot season, when producers put together new concepts for programming, hoping that one of what was back then the Big Three networks, would be sparked by an idea and pay for a sample show, or pilot. The resulting pile of pilots would then be pared down to the dozen or so that would actually be aired, and depending on the network's confidence in the potential ratings, a full season of twenty-six or a half season of thirteen shows would be ordered.

Pilot season is one of the busiest in Hollywood for actors, agents, producers, and network executives, and I got sucked right into the action along with everyone else. In the space of a few weeks I tried out for lead roles in two potential series. The first one pitted me against Patrick Wayne, the second against Desi Arnaz, Jr., and I lost out to both of them.

*   *   *

On the third, lightning struck. My life, in short, was about to take a steep climb into the show-business stratosphere, so high and so fast that I couldn't afford to look down without totally losing my balance, my perspective, and maybe even my sanity.

The pilot was being produced by Rick Rosner, one of television's most enduring and respected executives, who'd been at the helm of a lot of shows since the early sixties, most notably *240-Robert*. He was best known for cop dramas, and his new idea was right in line with his instincts for what people went for in a crime show: good-looking heroes, contemporary settings and situations, and lots of car chases and gunplay.

It was called *CHiPs*, short for California *Highway Patrol* and revolved around the adventures of two young motorcycle cops, a fair-haired kid named Jon Baker and his hot-tempered Italian side-kick, Frank "Ponch" Poncherello, named after a Vatican priest Rosner had known. Guess which one I was trying out for.

And it wasn't just me. For the initial casting sessions, Rosner and his partners had auditioned more than 250 hopefuls. But when I showed up, I didn't even have a chance to give them my "over-the-top" speech. Rosner, it turned out, had seen my work in *The New Centurions* and his gut instinct told him I might be right for the part. I could tell I was getting a very close inspection from the moment I walked in, so I just tried to do the best job I could with the scene they gave me.

"Very good" was all Rosner said after I'd finished. I had no way of knowing whether or not that was what he said to all the guys. But I got called back a day later and then a day after that. I could feel the stakes getting higher each time and I was starting to get keyed up. I wanted this job and the fat, steady paycheck that went with it.

The third time I went in to read my dialogue, which by then I could have said in my sleep, I was so nervous I missed a couple of my cues and muffed a couple of lines. I was so angry at myself for blowing something I knew so well that I slammed my fist into a nearby door.

"That's it!" shouted Rosner, jumping to his feet. "That's Ponch! That's the guy I want!" If I'd known it was going to be that easy I would have punched a whole lot more doors a whole lot sooner, believe me.

But, of course, nothing in Hollywood is ever that easy, and even though I had Rosner in my corner, there were still five other guys out of the original 250 who were still in contention for the part. More auditions followed until the competition was narrowed to me and another young actor, an Italian guy named Joe Nastassio. I saw myself at a disadvantage because the original script had called for Ponch to be Italian, but Joe actually didn't fit the part any better than I did, primarily because he had light skin and brown hair lighter than mine.

But there was one other hitch. One of Rosner's partners was concerned that because I'd played so many bad-guy roles in various other shows, people would have a hard time believing that I was now on the side of law and order. He insisted on having a screen test, decking me out in full police uniform and posing me next to a motorcycle to see if the image would change me from punk to protector. As I stood there under those hot lights I couldn't help thinking of Pete Panos and all the guys back at the precinct houses in the old neighborhood. If they could only see me now, a cop and an actor.

Well, I don't know whether it was that screen test, Rick Rosner's stubbornness, or my mother's prayers to the Virgin Mary, but I got the part and with it came an order for thirteen shows. The network wasn't exactly giving us an unqualified endorsement, but I didn't mind having to prove myself. After all, I had done it before . . . lots of times. So for the moment, I just savored the feeling. I was going to be Ponch.

*   *   *

There's probably not a more hopeful and optimistic bunch of people in the world than the cast and crew of a television series that has just gotten the green light to go ahead with production. Everything seems possible, no hurdle is too high, and a mantel full of Emmys is just a matter of a little luck and a lot of hard work. Everybody's primed to go, to give it their best and overlook any personality conflicts, private misgivings, and professional second-guessing that might get in the way of a successful first season.

I was certainly no different. I was determined to do my best and get along with everyone from the catering truck cook to my co-star. That co-star, cast in the role of Jon Baker, was a brash Wyoming native named Larry Wilcox, and from the moment we first shook hands, I tried my best to establish both a personal and professional bond. The truth is, I was a little awed by Larry from the outset. This guy was a genuine Westerner, a rugged individualist with a real cowboy image that extended to a pickup truck, complete with a gun rack in the cab and a saddle and bale of hay in the bed. He had really polished that portrait to a fine sheen, and the way he sauntered onto the set that first day was very impressive. "This guy is the real thing," I thought to myself. "He's got the walk and the talk. No wonder he got the role."

Then there was Robert Pine, who played the hard-bitten sergeant on the show, a guy who really considered himself a fine actor, a thespian in the finest tradition, and didn't let anyone forget it. I remember thinking at the time, "If he's such a big deal, what's he doing playing a supporting role on a cop show?" I never said anything, and as a matter of fact, he never said much to me, either. I always got the feeling that Pine was sort of holding himself back from us and from the show, waiting for a better offer to come his way.

The same wasn't true of Randi Oakes, who played the female cop on the show. Football great Joe Namath's former girlfriend, Randi had a modeling career before she got into acting. I appreciated her serious focus on the job, a brass-tacks attitude that I carried into all my work as well. I'd already been through the obligatory on-location romance with Jackie Giroux when we were together on *The Cross and the Switchblade* and had plenty of opportunities to put the moves on other actresses I'd worked with since then. I had found, though, that mixing business and pleasure in the movie industry just didn't work. There was too much professional jealousy, too many chances to let egos get in the way, and frankly, too much downtime to sit around the set and find silly things to argue about. I decided long ago to keep those two halves of my life separate.

Once the cast was in place, it was up to the writers, directors, and producers to put together a show that could sustain itself under the fierce competition of prime-time network television. As experienced as Rosner and his team might have been, anyone who produces a television series will tell you that the first season is pretty much hit-and-miss when it comes to finding a workable formula. Any show has to get its legs, to discover and play off the strength of dramatic situations and character interaction that may not be at all evident until what's in the script gets onto the screen. It's then that unexpected dynamics may emerge, and the personalities of characters really begin to take shape. What might have seemed like a minor point in the overall setup of the story can become the central pivot of the show.

The initial relationship between Ponch and Jon was clear from the moment I read the pilot script: Wilcox was the Lone Ranger and I was Tonto. It was a role I really didn't mind playing. A great sidekick, from the Green Hornet's Kato to Ralph Kramden's Ed Norton to Hopalong Cassidy's Red Conners, is a tried-and-true show-business formula, and I understood the second-banana concept as well as anyone.

But I can't say I thought Ponch, as originally written, was a great role. Rosner had conceived of a very buffoonish, goofy guy, always eating Twinkies and missing freeway exits during those weekly car chases we shot on stretches of under-construction L.A. freeway. While I also wouldn't say there was anything overtly racist in the way Ponch was supposed to be played, at the same time, he wasn't much of a credit to the Latinos who might have tuned in to the show to see one of their own. I would have preferred to see a character with a little more poise and intelligence, as motivated and dedicated as the Anglos around him. But I was there to do a job, and although I felt I could bring much more to my character, nobody was asking me.

But a funny thing happened from script to screen, and we all started to see it soon after the show began airing. Our initial time slot was Thursday nights at eight P.M., and while we weren't killing our competition in the ratings, we were holding our own, and then some. The decision was made to move us to Saturday nights, up against one of that season's comedy powerhouses, *Welcome Back, Kotter*. That show was created by Jimmy Komack, who had also been behind an earlier hit, *Chico and the Man*, and who would become a close friend.

Welcome Back, Kotter, of course, had John Travolta, a certified seventies phenomenon, in the role of the wisecracking Vinnie Barbarino. For the first six or eight shows, when we were in direct competition, we were really getting our clock cleaned, ratings-wise. But then came news that Travolta was leaving to pursue a movie career, and suddenly, over the course of the last few episodes of our first thirteen shows, we started pulling some big audience numbers.

The reason was pretty clear to me. The decade of the seventies saw a real jump in awareness of America's cultural diversity. That awareness was reflected in roles for ethnic actors, such as The Fonz and Barbarino, both hardcore Italians, and Ponch, who, at least at the beginning, was also supposed to be Italian. But even in that supposedly enlightened atmosphere of the mid-seventies, audiences couldn't really focus on more than one colorful minority character at a time. When Travolta was on *Kotter*, it was Barbarino. After he left, they turned their attention to Ponch.

I could see it reflected in the mail I started getting. Suddenly a handful of fan letters turned into sacks of mail addressed to Ponch. My character, regardless of how cartoonish I was required to play him, was connecting with viewers, and with that connection came some solid ratings points.

It didn't take long for Rosner and the network to pick up on what was happening out there in TV land. And Larry Wilcox couldn't help but notice either. Suddenly, it was Tonto riding in on a white horse, leaving the Lone Ranger in the dust. Even before we wrapped production on our first half season, a professional jealousy and personal rivalry began that would continue throughout the *CHiPs* years.

I can't say I really blame Larry all that much. After all, *CHiPs* was presented to him as a starring vehicle, and all of a sudden, an upstart was stealing his thunder. But at the same time, he could have handled the situation with a lot more grace and class. I knew the rule: The show must go on. Larry's attitude toward my sudden surge in popularity sometimes made it difficult to keep the show rolling. He'd show up late to rehearsals or act impatient if I missed a line. They were little things, but they started to add up, and the message was clear: He wasn't happy with the shift of attention to me.

As far as I was concerned, nothing was going to stop me from jumping through the window of opportunity that had opened up. I made myself available to every newspaper, magazine, and TV program that wanted to do a story on this fast-rising young Latino cop-show star, everything from Rona Barrett interviews to *Teen* and *Tiger Beat* magazine photo sessions. And it seems, looking through my scrapbook, as if the majority of those sessions must have been shot during very hot days because I always seemed to have my shirt off.

If I was being positioned as a sex symbol, well, that was just fine with me. As we came up on the tail end of those first thirteen episodes, the network still hadn't told us whether the show was going to be renewed. Like everyone else in the cast and crew of CHiPs, I wasn't sure how much longer the ride was going to last. I was determined to get as much mileage out of CHiPs for my own career as possible.

When I wasn't on the set, working long twelve- and fourteen-hour days, I'd be jetting around the country on a seemingly endless string of personal appearances, judging a country and western dance contest in Texas one night and eating Polish sausage at a Wisconsin state fair the next. I was willing to go anywhere they sent me, get my picture taken until I was blind from the flashbulbs, and sign autographs until my hand was numb. It was my shot at the big time and I wasn't going to let it pass me by.

Of course, in spite of all my hard work and the growing popularity of Ponch, the ultimate decision on the fate of CHiPs was out of my hands. We were all waiting with bated breath for word from the network. As the final weeks of our contract petered out, a gloom began to settle on the set, a feeling that the news, when it finally came, was going to be bad. That's just the way things are in Hollywood. For every "yes" you hear, there are a thousand "nos," and it's better to prepare yourself ahead of time for rejection than to let it surprise you.

I had other reasons for feeling depressed besides my uncertain future. Shortly after I started on CHiPs, I met a beautiful fashion model named Julie Swanson. We made the rounds of exclusive clubs, movie premieres, and celebrity functions together, and it was great to be seen around town with this gorgeous woman on my arm.

Unfortunately, that was about the only time we ever had together. If I wasn't out on some promotional tour, I would be up and gone by six in the morning for first call at the set. Then, immediately after wrapping for the day, I'd hightail it down to the studio to look at that day's footage, to check out my performance and to see what needed improving.

As a result, Julie just kind of drifted away, leaving for Europe to pursue her own career on the high-fashion circuit. We broke up three weeks before the last day of shooting, and by the time I got called for my final scene I was in a deep state of self-pity. My girl-friend had walked out on me and my show was about to shut down. The ride was over before it really began.

That last day, we were filming outside Los Angeles near Hansen Dam, a forlorn location in what seemed like the middle of nowhere. During a break I went back to my trailer and there, huddled in the shadows under the wheel, was the most forlorn bundle of fur I had ever seen. I went back to the catering truck for some food to lure out this half-starved and mange-ridden dog, and when I looked into his brown eyes, his world-weary expression seemed to sum up every-thing I was feeling.

I took that dog home with me, and the next day I took him to the local pet clinic. For the next few days, while I waited, hoping against hope, that Julie would change her mind and come back or that the show would be picked up, that dog and I were constant companions. We would sit on the sofa together while I played my favorite album from the great Brazilian artist, Gato Barbieri. The tune I kept dropping the needle on over and over was called "Don't Cry Rochelle," and it seemed to capture perfectly the miserable mood my canine companion and I shared.

One late night as I was listening to that cut for the twentieth time, I looked down at that poor skinny mutt in my lap and tried to offer what comfort I could. "Don't cry," I said. "Things have got to get better."

From that day on, the dog's name was Don't Cry, and from that day on, things did get better. A lot better.

Chapter Ten

When NBC finally came back with a decision to pick up the second half of its option for *CHiPs*, and we got the green light to finish the season, the gloom and doom that clouded my days disappeared like smog after a Santa Ana wind.

We were back in business and I threw myself into my work with more energy and enthusiasm than ever. When I got the news, I rushed down to Rosner's office on the MGM lot and burst in, shouting "Let's celebrate!"

After Rosner got over his surprise at having a crazed actor barge in on him, he reached for his wallet and pulled out some bills. "Okay," he said with a smile. "Why don't you go down to the store and buy us a bottle of champagne?"

I looked at the money in his hands for a moment before taking it. Heading for the door, I turned back to him on my way out.

"Mr. Rosner?" I said politely.

He looked up from his desk, still smiling.

"I'll go out and get the groceries, but this is the last time you send this particular spic on your errands."

The look of shock on his face was just what I'd been aiming for and I laughed out loud. After a moment he joined in, but I think he got the message behind my little joke. I knew, and I wanted him to know, that *CHiPs* was back on the air because, at least in part, Ponch had struck a chord with the viewers. I was his ace in the hole.

It wasn't ego that brought me to that conclusion, it was the response of fans across the country. The show had sparked because people found a likable character they could relate to, and that, as much as anything, is the key to long-running success in television.

It was a fact quickly grasped at the network as well. As a result, as we finished up our second run of thirteen shows, we began to see sure signs of change on the set and in the production office.

The most notable was in Rosner's role as creator and producer. The network was concerned about consistent budget overruns and seemed less than happy with the tone of the scripts that were being turned in under Rosner's direction. It was the same concern I had secretly felt for some time; the show had a thin and two-dimensional feel to it and Ponch was still being played pretty much for laughs.

By the time we heard that *CHiPs* would go on for a second year, those changes had become reality. Rosner was taken off the show, replaced by a veteran TV producer named Sy Shermack. With Rosner's departure, many of his handpicked creative staff and technical crew also packed their bags, their jobs now being filled by Shermack's handpicked favorites. It was another tried-and-true Hollywood tradition: When you go, your people go with you.

I was sorry to see Rosner get the boot, especially from a show he had nurtured from the ground up. He was a personal friend, even though we were sometimes at odds over the direction of the show. I knew he'd be set financially with the royalties he'd be getting as the show's creator, but I could still understand the anger and bitterness he felt when they took his baby away.

On the other hand, there was no question that Shermack ran a much tighter ship. As a seasoned professional he knew how to bring TV productions in on time and on budget, and more important, his staff of writers began making some long overdue adjustments in Ponch's character.

Of course, this meant that I was taking more and more of a central role in the series, and as a result, relations between Larry Wilcox and me continued to deteriorate. Knowing how he felt, I did my best to stay on friendly terms and, when that didn't work, to keep my distance. It wasn't long before the set was divided into two camps, Larry's people and my people. There were constant low-level hassles as the factions tried to get the best of each other, down to such trivial moves as grabbing all the seats in the shade for the lunch break. I tried my best not to let Larry push my buttons, even when I felt my people were being abused. Whenever the tension between us spilled out into the open, I made it my policy to just smile and nod and keep my cool.

Larry and I never really had much of a relationship off the set. We didn't hang out together or share our downtime. But I never had a problem making friends, and the fact was, I felt a lot more comfortable with some of the crew members than I did with some of the cast.

They were guys I could really relate to, hard workers, who put in an honest day for an honest dollar, and they were the ones who, in time, would prove to be the best and most loyal friends. Among them was my stunt double, Danny Rogers, a quiet, unassuming guy who could do everything from popping wheelies on a Harley to hang-gliding to bareback riding.

Another crew regular I got close to was Bill Young, the CHiPs car wrangler, who was in charge of all the vehicles for the show. They were the guys I'd eat lunch, gossip between takes, and have a few beers with as the production schedule started to settle into a predictable routine.

I also made it a point to be as friendly as possible with the stars who would do guest appearances on the show. Among the many was Ed McMahon, a warm and wonderful man whom I consider to be one of my best friends in Hollywood. We first met when I noticed that the trailer they had given him on the set was one of the small, standard-issue variety instead of the deluxe accommodations provided for Larry and me. It seemed positively rude to treat a star of Ed's stature that way, and I insisted that he take my quarters for the duration of the shoot. It was the beginning of a long and cordial friendship that included regular lunches at Ma Maison and even occasional business and pleasure trips to New York with him and his wife, Victoria.

By the beginning of our second season, CHiPs was really starting to fire on all cylinders, thanks in part to NBC's decision to put the show in one of the most coveted time slots in the whole weekly schedule. Sunday night at eight P.M., was the old Bonanza hour and the perfect time to catch audiences, after dinner and before bed. All they wanted was to settle down after the weekend and get ready for the beginning of a new week. As a result, our ratings began a steady climb, until we were consistently beating the competition and were lodged firmly in the top-five listings.

At the same time, it was becoming increasingly clear, from all the mail and the market research that the network did, that Ponch was CHiPs's main attraction. It was a reality reflected in a nickname that I picked up on the set. Whenever I was needed for a shot, and whoever the director was that week would call for me, the crew would shout out, "Where's The Money? Get The Money over here." I was The Money, the guy who was buttering the bread, the one who kept the wheels greased and rolling. I guess I could have taken it as an insult, but to me it was just a fact that without Ponch CHiPs would have folded.

Shooting on the demanding schedule of an hour-long weekly TV series took up almost all my time. It wasn't unusual for me to simply sleep in my trailer, out on such well-known location sites as Vasquez Rocks, after an exhausting day of work. But even in the midst of a round-the-clock whirl of alternately filming and promoting the show, I still tried to squeeze in a real life for myself.

The first thing I did after hearing we'd been renewed for a second season was to generally upgrade my lifestyle. I moved out of my little one-bedroom place and bought a condo that I decorated exactly to my specifications, for a tropical feel, wicker furniture and lots of breezy, bright colors. I was beginning to discover that I really liked to express another creative side of myself by picking fabrics and furniture that said something about my personality. In my choice of a new car I also displayed a taste for colors that stood out and made a statement. I bought another Mercedes, a cute little two-door 450 SL, tan with a bamboo-highlighted interior.

But even as I was finding ways to have a good time with my newfound wealth, I wanted to make sure the people I cared about were provided for. It was one thing for the crew of CHiPs to call me The Money. I wanted to let my family know that The Money was there for them, too.

Early on in our second season, I bought a beautiful house for my mother—three bedrooms, gated, with a circular drive—in the hills above Tarzana. In a family that had struggled for so long without the protection and guidance of a real father, I wanted to be able to take on that role myself, to give my mother and Carmen and Joey what we'd all been missing for so long.

Well, my mom lasted in that place about three weeks. A native New Yorker who had never learned to drive, she was miserable in her lavish new surroundings. "I can't even go to the market for milk, Papo," she wailed. It did no good for me to offer to buy her a car and get her driving lessons, or even hire a private chauffeur. She wanted to be back where she felt comfortable, and in the end, all I really wanted was for her to be happy. So I bought her a nice apartment in New York on East Fifty-seventh Street and let her go.

Carmen and Joey, on the other hand, jumped at the chance to get a taste of the good life in California. Since I still owned the spacious Tarzana house, I suggested Joey and his family move in, paying three hundred dollars in rent while I picked up what was left of the mortage payment. I also put in a few calls around town and landed Joey a job as a publicity photographer at NBC, where he still works.

I also did my best to set Carmen up, getting her bit parts on CHiPs and always making sure to touch her or talk to her if we were in a scene together. Under the rules of the extras union, anyone who gets spoken to or makes physical contact with a principal player in a production gets an extra two hundred and fifty dollars, and it was a great way to put some cash in my sister's pocket.

Carmen had just left her husband, Myron, and although they would later get back together, right about then she was interested in starting a new life in Los Angeles. It was something I was starting to look for as well.

Despite all the success I was enjoying, I couldn't seem to make up for the lack of a meaningful relationship since Julie Swanson left. Part of the problem, of course, was that as the young star of a hit action-adventure series, most connections I made with women were of the hot, heavy, and brief variety.

As CHiPs continued to dominate the season, the number of beautiful, willing, and able young ladies making themselves available seemed to expand geometrically. It was like being a kid running wild in the aisles of Toys "R" Us: so much to choose, so little time. It was a fast and loose lifestyle that was very much in keeping with the times. More than once I would take one girl out on a date and end up with another before the night was over. We'd hop from party to party across L.A., from Mulholland Drive overlooking the sparkling lights of the Valley, to Malibu, where someone was always swimming nude in the cool night water.

Sure, I did my share of questionable substances in those days, snorting a line of coke if it was offered or toasting some new romance with a bottle of Dom Pérignon. That was what the seventies was all about—flying to Studio 54 for the weekend and driving down to Malibu in my Mercedes for a beach party at The Colony. When women threw themselves at me, I never really stopped to think, "Gee, is this the one I want to settle down with for the rest of my life?" I simply went for what was being offered and then moved along to the next tempting display.

But even in the middle of that heady, intoxicating era, there was a part of me that was looking for something more. Forbidden fruit, whether sex or drugs or just the knowledge that I could get away with anything, lost its luster when I realized that nothing was stopping me. I would have never allowed myself to get too deeply into any drug—I had seen what addiction could do to a man—and after a while, sex with strangers, no matter how beautiful and accommodating, was just like any other addiction.

I needed someone special in my life, someone to depend on and someone to depend on me. It was inevitable. As much as I was moving smoothly down the Hollywood fast lane, the values that my mother had instilled in me, those simple truths of virtue and morality and responsibility, still tugged at my sleeve. Maybe I wasn't ready to get married and raise a family, but I sure needed something more than an endless succession of fleeting, fawning faces.

I found that special person when I did an appearance on a Dick Clark special where one of the extras caught my eye. Kathy Lautner and I dated steadily over the next two years. We were closer than friends but never close enough to make a lasting commitment to each other.

Kathy was seventeen when we first met, a model and actress with big career ambitions of her own. She had very special qualities about her, sweet and generous, but underneath she nursed the wounds of an abusive upbringing.

As much as anything, we just clung together during that time, looking for a safe haven amid all the uncertainty while reaching for the brass ring of stardom, trying our best to make some kind of life together. She moved into my condo and it was great while it lasted. I think I came as close to loving her as I was capable of during those crazed and confusing years. In the end, it was our careers that we were married to and the time it might have taken to build something strong and lasting was already spoken for. When Kathy, like Julie before her, finally drifted away, I was too busy to notice the empty place in my life she left behind.

CHiPs had gone from being the chance of a lifetime to a daily grind consisting of an unending string of repeated lines, stage directions, and on-demand emotions. It was a routine we tried to break any way we could.

For example, Larry Wilcox and I raised a stink about being towed around on our cycles on the back of a camera car. Shermack, it seems, was concerned that his stars might hurt themselves if we actually drove the bikes. We felt like such dorks, dressed in full uniform and being hauled around like kids on a carnival ride, that we insisted on freewheeling the big Kawasakis.

We finally got our way after we took a complete course in motorcycle safety from Scott Wilson, an instructor from the CHP Academy in Sacramento. Before he was done, I could ride that bike perfectly and even pull off some fancy figure eights. We always had a professional California Highway Patrol technical adviser on the set, which served to remind me again that I was more than just playing a role in a TV show—for a lot of people, kids especially, I was a role model. Just as Pete Panos had given me an example to follow when I was young, I wanted to help other kids, who might be looking for some direction in their lives, to do something worth-while.

It was a responsibility that I took very seriously, even though I didn't always follow through in my private life. Yet, with the sched-ule I was keeping, I really didn't have much of a private life to speak of. If I wasn't on the set working, I was in the gym keeping in shape or at some function set up by the studio. Most of those appearances were strictly for promotional purposes, but I was proud to participate in some. I lent my time and energies to charities like Make-a-Wish Foundation and Toys for Tots, and made hospital visits to kids whenever I could. It felt great to use celebrity and star power for something that might actually help someone. I was also involved for a short time in a Hispanic community-awareness organization called Nosotros. They named me Best Actor in a Series, which, in retrospect, was pretty ironic because, at the time, I was virtually the only Hispanic actor in a series. The problem with Nosotros and similar associations built around ethnic identity, I discovered, was the amount of infighting and politics that went on. I would offer my services, only to discover that such organizations were split into Mexican, Puerto Rican, or Central American factions, each one trying to get a spokesman to represent their slice of the ethnic pie. It really left a bad taste in my mouth and it would be many more years before my identity as a Latino finally had a chance to find its full expression.

There was no question about it, during those first few seasons of CHiPs, I was flying high, barely stopping to catch my breath. Some-thing had to give, and when it did, like almost everything else that seems to happen in my life, it was in spectacular fashion.

Chapter Eleven

The whole house of cards I so painstakingly built would collapse suddenly and completely at the beginning of our third season of CHiPs. Looking back, I guess I would have to say it was inevitable that, sooner or later, I'd hit some kind of brick wall.

My faith in God can basically be summed up by saying I believe He helps those who help themselves. But it sometimes seems that He also steps in with a bit of divine intervention when you've forgotten not only how to apply the brakes on your own life, but even where the brakes are. Success and money and easy access to the best things Hollywood had to offer had sent me so high, I was bound to crash sooner or later. I just wish the head-on collision with destiny hadn't been quite so literal.

It was late on a Friday afternoon, the end of the day at the end of a week shooting the first show of the third season. The episode was called "Roller Disco," guest-starring Larry Storch, my old friend from *Airport 1975*, as one of the crooks. Everyone was rushing to get in the final shots before the light faded, and we had just finished a simple stunt that involved me and Larry chasing the bad guys down an alley on our bikes.

We rehearsed the scene and shot it without a hitch. The director was Don Wise and when he yelled, "Print it!" I headed for my trailer and a nice long shower. But I had only gotten my shirt off before there was a knock on the door, and when I opened it, some gofer told me that there had been a hair on the camera lens and we were going to have to do the scene again.

"Great," I thought. "Just what I need." But duty was calling, so I climbed back into my uniform and returned to the set.

By that time the light was really waning fast. We had to get the shot right away or go into another day, which meant going over budget. The stuntmen, experienced drivers who handled the car-chase sequences, had all gone home. The decision was made to use a teamster to do the stunt driving. They found a young kid who happened to be hanging around the lot waiting to drive his truck home.

Everyone took their places as Don yelled, "Action!" and the cameras began to roll. It was a strictly routine sequence. Larry and I were supposed to run out of a warehouse, jump on our bikes, and chase a car that was backing down the alley in reverse and out of the shot. I must have done scenes like it a hundred times before.

The kid behind the wheel, with the camera in the seat next to him, took off with a squeal of peeling rubber, just as he'd been told. The only problem was, no one told him where his stop mark was, and when he decided he'd gone far enough, he just slammed on the brakes.

I must have been about ten feet away from him. There was never a chance for me to even think about slowing down, much less stopping. The only clear thought I remember having was that the hood of that car was coming up awfully fast. The next thing I knew I was sprawled out across it, slamming head-on into the bumper at thirty-five miles an hour.

After a moment, I slid off onto the pavement as bright black lights began popping in front of my eyes. I felt somehow removed, distant from the disaster that had just happened, and I found myself wondering if I'd broken anything.

I had. My wrist was shattered and twelve ribs were fractured, which in turn had punctured and collapsed both lungs. The black lights got bigger and brighter as I heard a loud noise in my ears. "What's that?" I thought, before realizing that the sound was coming from me in the futile effort to breathe. Meanwhile, the crew came running up and gathered around me and Larry knelt down next to me, asking over and over again, "Who am I? Who am I?" He had been to Vietnam and, knowing that going into shock could well be fatal in a situation like mine, was trying his best to keep me conscious and aware.

No matter what our differences might have been, then or later, I'll always be grateful for the care and concern he showed that afternoon. He continued to talk to me and held my hand until a Sheriff's helicopter arrived and I was hoisted onto a stretcher for a quick trip to UCLA Medical Center.

After that it was all just a blur of half-remembered impressions and a searing pain that radiated from my chest in concentric rings of pure agony. Vague recollections of being lifted onto a bed and having my clothes cut away are mixed with memories of my own voice shouting obscenities as they probed my vein with a needle, preparing to inject dye to determine whether my aorta had been ruptured. I must have been struggling and thrashing against the nurses because, in one vivid moment, I remember an orderly leaning over me and saying, very calmly, "Hey, man, if you don't cool it . . . you're going to die."

That hit home and I stopped fighting as an Asian doctor hurried up with two clear plastic tubes in his hands. Without saying a word he took one tube and, after making an incision, shoved it past my shattered ribs and into my lungs to drain the blood. Before I could even scream, he did the same thing on my other side. And that's when I passed into a blessed darkness, free of pain and the terrible fear that I might never wake up again.

Of course, I did wake up, even though in the condition in which I found myself, all I wanted to do was to fall back into that dark oblivion. I was, to put it simply, in a world of pain and would remain in the Intensive Care Unit at UCLA hospital for five days, breathing oxygen in a tent, with tubes stuck in me from every angle. I was constantly passing in and out of consciousness, trying to wrap my mind around exactly what had happened to me and slowly coming to the realization that I had come as close to death as any man could without actually crossing over to the other side forever.

In fact, I almost did cross over. Those first couple of days were really touch and go, the doctors told me later. As a precaution they had notified my mother back in New York. They monitored me constantly as my vital signs hovered at the edge of flatlining and it still wasn't clear whether I would pull through.

It must have been shortly after dawn of the fourth day when I opened my eyes, swimming up out of the deep pool of those numbing painkillers, blinking back at the bright fluorescent light from the fixtures on the ceiling. I must have moaned, because suddenly faces began appearing next to the bed: my mother and her longtime boyfriend, Andre, and Bill Tarman, an old friend of mine from my extra days in New York. As I turned my head to look around I even saw my father, sitting pale and shriveled in his wheelchair.

What happened next is as clear to me as words on this page. I sat up in the bed and, seeing that my mother was crying, said, "Hey, Mom, don't worry . . . everything's okay. I'm gonna be fine." It didn't seem as if she heard me, so I turned to the others in the room.

"It's great to see you all," I said with a smile. "You came all the way out from New York to be here with me?" No response. It was as if I were invisible. So I got out of bed and walked right up to them. "Hey," I said, puzzled and starting to get a little frightened, "it's me. Mom, Dad . . . look, don't you recognize me?" They were staring right through me, looking back toward the bed, so naturally I turned around to see what they were so interested in.

It was then that I saw myself, or at least my body, lying on the bed. There I was, inside that oxygen tent, with tubes still stuck in me and those gleaming machines beeping quietly as they tracked my feeble vital signs. "That's me," I thought to myself. "I'm still in that bed. But then . . . what am I doing standing here looking at myself?"

I didn't have any answers then, and I don't have any now. All I knew was that the feeling of being in two places at the same time, looking at my own body and watching my family stare down at me like it was my last hour on earth, was a scene that would stay with me forever. I somehow knew that if I didn't get back into my bed, and my body, I might never return to the land of the living, so I turned around and stepped onto the sheets and into my skin.

Was I just delirious or was I having a real out-of-body experience? Was it a dream or did I step into eternity for just that moment? I can't say for sure, but I also can't shake the feeling that if I hadn't turned around and seen myself, and if I hadn't, right then and there, returned to my own flesh and blood, I might still be roaming the halls of UCLA to this day, a lonely ghost in a flapping hospital gown.

If you asked my opinion, I'd have to say that my will to live was too strong to surrender. I still had things I wanted to do, whole chapters of my life that still needed to be written. Checking out just wasn't an option, and while I'm not suggesting that my willpower was enough to stall death, I do believe that we've all got an appointed time to meet our maker, and that mine just hadn't come.

Of course, the serious injuries I sustained might have settled the issue regardless of my personal timetable, but because I was taking such good care of myself, I think I had the strength and stamina to match my desire to live. I'd been working out on a daily basis, practicing karate and pumping iron every morning down at Vince's

Gym. I was probably in the best shape of my life, and that made all the difference in my pulling through.

The day after the supernatural encounter with myself, my condition improved so much that the doctors pulled me out of intensive care. After that, I was out of the woods and it was just a matter of allowing time for my body to heal itself.

Patience, however, has never been one of my virtues, and I'm sure if you ask the nurses on my floor who was the worst patient they ever had to deal with, I'd probably make the top five.

As soon as I was well enough to sit up and talk, I had a steady stream of visitors in and out of my room and there were news crews camped outside twenty-four hours a day, waiting for medical updates. It was the biggest thing that had happened in the hospital, the nurses told me, since John Wayne had checked in, and they made sure to bring in every newspaper and magazine with my near-death story splashed over the cover.

The crowds of friends and well-wishers and the constant glare of media attention was something I could handle. After all, I had been doing it for so long that being a celebrity, even one in a hospital bed, came naturally.

What I couldn't handle so easily were the times when I was left alone, late at night, after visiting hours were over and the only things to keep me company were the soft noises and muted lights of all the medical hardware around my bed. It's an old story that anyone who has a brush with death finds a new perspective on life, and I was no exception. I had a lot of time on my own to think during those long nights in the hospital, more time to myself than I'd had in years. I had the opportunity to play back, at a slower speed, the blinding pace of my professional life and the steep ups and downs of my personal life.

The more I thought about it, the more I realized how much events had controlled me instead of the other way around. I had learned from the streets of Spanish Harlem to move fast and decisively in any situation and it had become a habit for me to act first and ask questions later. As I lay there, feeling my tender ribs and battered lungs ache in time to my beating heart, it seemed as if there had never been a moment I could remember when I hadn't had my fists up, fighting someone or something for what I wanted or what I thought I deserved.

And what did I have to show for it? I was the star of a hit television show, a familiar face to millions of people across the country, a certified star with all the perks and pleasures that go along with the job. But what could I really call my own? That little yellow Mercedes? That was leased. My condo? Rented. My bank account may have been fat, but what satisfaction was all that money giving me? I loved the work I did, but I knew that, in Hollywood, you're only as good as your ratings and what goes up inevitably comes down, sometimes with a shattering crash.

What was I doing with my life? In twenty years would I still be picking up willing young ladies on the dance floor of Studio 54, jetting around the country for one more personal appearance, suiting up as Ponch for one more freeway chase? Not likely.

I was beginning to understand that the things that really mattered in life—family, children, a wife—I'd been putting on hold for too long. It was a realization that led to a deep sense of depression, a state I was totally unfamiliar with. I had always been a fighter, always optimistic about what tomorrow would bring. Suddenly I was facing the fact that tomorrow might turn out a lot less rosy than I'd envisioned, that there might come a day when all I had to show for my life was a tattered book of press clippings and an occasional second look from a passerby, wondering where he had seen my face before.

From depression it was a short step to self-pity and by the time I was finally released from the hospital, I was feeling pretty sorry for myself. I wasn't sure what needed to change, or how to go about it, but I was damned sure something was going to be different from that moment on.

Looking back, I have to say that I'm convinced it should be mandatory for anyone who's had a serious accident or life-threatening event in their lives to receive psychological therapy. It's one thing to allow time for the body to heal, but the mind has its own process of rehabilitation that it must go through. That's just as important as getting a patient out of bed and walking under his own steam. I didn't have the chance to absorb what had happened to me, much less to understand how it had impacted my life.

And that was nobody's fault but my own. Sure, there was pressure from the show to get back to work. Sure, I was restless and felt more than ready to pull out those tubes and get out of that backless dressing gown. But I really wasn't ready, not in my mind or spirit. I needed to take it easy, to reach down and try to grapple with all the emotions that I'd been ignoring for so long. But I just assumed that all I really had to do was pick up where I'd left off. I didn't know how wrong I could be.

The first thing I did was move into a rented apartment on Doheny Drive in West Hollywood. My condo seemed cold and empty when I arrived there my first day out of the hospital. All that remained was memories of a life that seemed to have been lived by someone else and, right then, what I yearned for more than anything was a fresh start. Even then, I think I was looking for a way to change the life I had almost lost, but I just didn't know where to begin.

A few days after my discharge, while I was still on sick leave from the show, I got a call from Bob Munson, who was the teamster captain on the CHiPs location.

"Erik," he said, "I just want you to know how sorry I am that one of my guys put you in the hospital. And I don't want you to worry. We're getting rid of the kid who was driving that car."

"Hey, wait a minute," I replied, wincing from the effort of talking and feeling my busted ribs throb with each word. "It wasn't his fault. He's just a kid. He didn't know what he was doing. The last thing I want is to put all this on him. You let him keep his job."

Munson agreed, but as I hung up the phone I realized just how angry I was at the carelessness and negligence that had almost killed me. Up until that moment I just counted myself lucky to be alive. Suddenly, I wanted to get back at whoever had put me so directly in harm's way.

And that was Ed Montanus, the head of MGM TV, the man ultimately responsible for everything that happens and doesn't happen on the company's productions. Ed was basically a very decent guy, big and jovial, with a personality to match. But when he showed up one day shortly after I'd returned to work, I directed all my frustration and suppressed anger right in his face.

"Everyone calls me The Money," I shouted, stomping around in those big police boots on the dusty set. "Well, is this the way you treat your money? You just about wasted me for the sake of getting one more shot and staying on budget. Well, let me tell you something. I'm not going to forget how I've been treated. Someone's going to pay."

When I'd finished my tirade, with the cast and crew standing around like innocent bystanders at the scene of a car crash, Ed just looked at me and said, in that deep, calm voice of his, "What can we do to make it up to you, Erik?"

"What can you do?" I repeated at the top of my lungs. "What can you do?" The truth was, I didn't know what they could do, but I was sure as hell going to think of something. I knew that, behind all this care and concern, was the real fear that I'd drag them into a lawsuit, which I really had no intention of doing. I was more interested in keeping my job than being compensated for what was, after all, an accident. But I sure didn't want Ed Montanus to know that.

"You want to make me happy?" I finally said. "You want to make nice and have me back on the job like a good employee?"

"More than anything" was Ed's evenhanded reply.

"Then buy me a Rolls-Royce," I snapped, saying the first thing that popped into my head. "A beautiful Rolls-Royce and have it sitting in my driveway tomorrow morning."

And that's exactly what they did. I woke up the next day to find a gleaming yellow Corniche parked in front of my apartment. "This is more like it," I thought, as I sat in the plush leather seat and felt the noiseless vibration of the engine through the steering wheel. "This is what I call a get-well present."

Actually, I couldn't have cared less about a fancy new car. The last thing I needed was another set of wheels. What I wanted was to know that I was valued and that people wouldn't ever take me, or my well-being, for granted again. The Rolls was just a way of letting them know how I felt.

But while that Rolls might have gone a long way to soothe my ruffled feelings, it did just the opposite for my co-star, Larry Wilcox.

Larry's resentment and jealousy had been brewing ever since the beginning of the second season, and it was understandable. He was going through a difficult divorce at the time, even while his position as the Lone Ranger to my Tonto was getting more turned around with each episode.

Aside from the sacks of fan mail addressed to me that poured in week after week, I was also grabbing the lion's share of the media attention that always surrounds a hit show. I remember once walking past a news rack in my neighborhood supermarket and seeing a dozen different photos of my face staring back from magazine covers. Larry was conspicuous only by his absence. Part of the problem, I think, was that he had developed a childish fixation on the helmet and sunglasses that were part of our regular CHiPs costume and was rarely photographed without them. Consequently, people weren't really sure what he looked like, while I, on the other hand, was only too willing to let them get a good long look at me.

By the time I returned to the set after the accident, riding in on the tidal wave of publicity that surrounded it, the situation had gone from bad to worse. We could get through our scenes together without incident. After all, that was our job. But as soon as the director called "cut" we'd head off in different directions without saying another word to each other that wasn't written in a script.

I always did my best not to let him bother me. But when personal friends and co-workers got the butt end of his abuse, such as having to do more than their share of work or getting chewed out in front of everyone for some minor infraction, the result, more often than not, was a shouting match that the unit publicist would have to work overtime to keep out of the press.

The bad blood between me and Larry finally spilled out over that Rolls-Royce the studio had bought to placate me. When I drove it onto the set the next day, I could see Larry through my tinted windows doing a slow burn. I later found out that on that same afternoon, he had hightailed it to his agent and raised such a stink that the agent, in turn, got on the hot line to Montanus's office.

"Be reasonable," Montanus pleaded with Larry. "We gave the car to Erik to try and make up for the accident."

"I don't care" was Larry's reply. "If he gets one, then I get one."

And he did. It was then that I realized I was never going to get on the right side of Larry Wilcox. He was a co-worker, and while we had to do the best we could to make the show the best it could be, I knew as soon as I saw him drive up his own Corniche that we would never be friends while CHiPs was on the air. In our better moments together, I considered us part of the same team. Today I consider Larry a good friend. But at that moment, I understood clearly that it was every man for himself and that Larry's only concern was to have a place on a bandwagon that was now being pulled by yours truly.

Chapter Twelve

If a bad attitude from Larry Wilcox was all I'd had to deal with at the time, I'm sure I could have handled it with a minimum of personal inconvenience. After all, I'd dealt with harder cases than Larry, just trying to keep myself alive in the projects. As disillusioned as I was by his power games and one-upmanship, I had a job to do and I was determined to do it.

But Larry was the least of my problems. It seemed as if the accident was like some sort of thread that, once it had been pulled, began to unravel the rest of my life, both personally and professionally.

Beneath the smooth-running surface of the CHiPs production, I had been making a few career moves that had resulted in some very ruffled feathers.

The biggest bird that I'd bothered was my agent, Jack Fields. When Jack's agency had first landed me the job on CHiPs, I was more than happy to accept the standard contract for a starring role in an unproven series: five thousand dollars an episode. More than a fair deal, it seemed to me then like manna dropped straight out of heaven. I was doing what I loved to do, and getting paid top dollar for it.

Of course, by the time the second season rolled around and CHiPs had gone from being just another cop show to the hottest thing on the tube, I went back to Jack to ask how he was going to maximize our advantage. His answer was both what I wanted, and what I didn't want to hear. If nothing else, Jack had that patented agent's talent of making bad news sound good.

"Erik," he told me. "It's too soon to make a big move yet. The show looks like it's picking up steam, but you never know. I think we should go for the standard contract, seventy-five hundred a week for the second season, and if things keep going the way they have, we'll move in for the big bucks in the third season."

How big? Jack threw around some pretty impressive figures, anywhere from $25,000 to $35,000 a show, and that too sounded simply too good to pass up. So, at his suggestion, I hung back and took the standard fee of $7,500 per show for the entire second season.

Halfway through the year, however, it became evident even to me that I was worth a whole lot more. Aside from my weekly appearances on CHiPs, I had co-hosted a variety show with one of my all-time favorites, Dean Martin, appeared on Merv Griffin and Dinah! done a couple of Bob Hope specials, and landed a regular slot on Hollywood Squares. I'd been nominated for a People's Choice Award and had my own fan club, which did a brisk business in posters. The fan mail was now up to over four thousand letters a week. It was the big time.

But in the interim, Jack had been having more than a few power lunches with the MGM TV honchos. Of course, I'll never really know what went on behind those closed doors. But, if you want my opinion, they had cooked up a deal that left me out of the loop entirely.

I think that because Jack Fields handled a huge roster of actors through his agency, the MGM executives may have made him an offer he couldn't refuse. If he held the line on salaries, all his clients would work. He'd be getting his 10 percent from each con-

tract he brokered, which, considering how many actors he represented, would add up to a whole lot more than getting the same
commission from only a few clients, no matter how big their salaries
were.

The MGM angle would also have been straightforward. As with
any successful television show, the real money was not in the first
run of the series. Rather, it was in selling syndication rights. Syn-
dicating a show, which simply means selling old episodes to independent stations, is a virtual license to print greenbacks. There are
no up-front production costs, and the only real expense is in residual
payments to the principal creative participants—actors, writers, directors, and producers. Even those payments diminish with each
year the series stays in syndication.

The usual length of time a show has to run before it can qualify
for syndication is five seasons. By then there are enough episodes
in the can to make the package worth selling. CHiPs was entering
its third season, which meant that MGM would have to create original programs for only two more seasons before it could close up the
shop and start selling the show in perpetual reruns.

The bottom line of all this was, well . . . the bottom line. For all
the money that flows in and out of Hollywood, no one is anxious
to part with a penny more than they have to, and the prospect of
my taking anything more than the standard salary for that third
season, no matter how brightly my star was shining, just irked the
executives. If nothing else, it simply created a precedent for other
hot young stars to follow, so it was vitally important for them to
hold the line.

Jack, who, after all, was getting paid to represent my best interests, might have just rolled over when it came to the not-so-subtle
suggestions of the MGM TV brass. What I know for sure is that,
when the time came around to begin negotiating for my third-
season salary, he announced with a straight face that, all things

considered, it was probably best for everyone concerned if I just agreed to the standard contract, which was only a slight bump to eight thousand dollars.

Needless to say, I hit the roof. I hadn't been the one who had been promised the moon if the show took off, but once Jack had started talking in five figures, I got used to that concept very quickly. All of a sudden, there he was knocking me back down into the bush leagues.

"I'm sorry, Erik," he said, "but the studio just isn't going to go for a nickel more."

"Then you go in and fight for me," I insisted.

"I tried," he said, throwing up his hands. "Look, Erik . . . you don't want to make waves with these guys."

But waves were exactly what I wanted to make. "Okay, Jack," I said, after taking a deep breath and counting to ten, "you just step back and stay out of the way. I'll handle this myself."

"What are you going to do?" he asked, alarmed. But by that time I was already out the door.

My first stop was Rick Rosner. I knew there was no love lost between Rick and the studio because, even though he was getting a healthy chunk of change as the creator of CHiPs, it had taken his baby away from him and given it to someone else. He never had a chance to nurture his own show, and now that it was a major hit, his removal stung even more.

"Rick," I said, when we sat down together, "who's the toughest lawyer in this town?"

He knew the answer and I knew that he knew, because Henry Bushkin was a personal friend of his. If the name Bushkin sounds familiar, it should. Anybody who watched Johnny Carson on *The Tonight Show* over his thirty-year run heard Johnny refer again and again to his lawyer, "Bombastic Bushkin." Same guy.

Rick was only too willing to put me in touch with Bushkin. Bushkin, in turn, was only too willing to take my case. He knew what everyone else knew: CHiPs was a hit because people loved Ponch. I was Ponch, which meant that without me, there was no CHiPs.

It was as simple as that, and apparently Bombastic Bushkin didn't have too much trouble pointing out the obvious to the MGM king-pins. As attorney for both me and Johnny Carson, Bushkin represented the two highest-rated shows on NBC and a quick call to David Begelman, who was running the network at the time, convinced everybody concerned that giving Estrada what he wanted was the right and fair thing to do.

In fact, it was so right and so fair that instead of the $25,000 or $35,000 that Jack had tossed off, Bushkin landed me a cool $50,000 an episode.

I had won the battle, but the war still raged on. When Larry Wilcox caught wind of my astronomical salary hike, he insisted on a matching raise for himself under what's called a "favored nations" clause in our contract, which stipulates that, as co-stars, we were to have parity in every aspect of our work.

I didn't mind, I'd gotten what I believed I really deserved. How they treated Larry Wilcox was none of my business.

What was my business, on the other hand, was the way Jack Fields handled the situation. Of all the twists and turns of this sad saga, his reaction struck me as the most ludicrous. Jack had been ready for me to settle for a measly $8,000 an episode. And now he was asking for his cut of a $50,000 paycheck, a neat $5,000 a week.

My response to Jack's modest proposal was two simple words: No Way. Actually, I added a few more words just to get the point across, but that was the main idea. Jack was equally direct in his reply. He threatened to sue me.

I called his bluff and we ended up in arbitration, where Jack regaled the judge with a long and fanciful tale, the gist of which was that if it hadn't been for the hard work of Fields and Associates, Erik Estrada would still be the nobody he was when he first knocked on their door, instead of the nationally known TV star that he was today. The truth was, I never even hired Jack until I'd landed the CHiPs job, which was a fact he conveniently left out of his long sob story.

It was a story the judge took about thirty seconds to consider before throwing Jack's tale back at him and handing me the decision. I had won and was obligated to pay Jack 10 percent only on the salary he would have negotiated—eight thousand dollars—an episode which came down to a paltry eight hundred in his pocket every week.

But Jack wasn't finished. He appealed the decision and when he lost a second time, he tried for a third. It was only when he finally struck out for good that he gave up.

I had won. Sort of. While I may have gotten the salary I thought I deserved and while I might have beaten my agency and the studio at their own game, it was a victory that came with a steep price . . . one I didn't realize I had to pay until it was too late.

Ask people in Hollywood today what they remember best about Erik Estrada and I'll give you odds that while many will bring up CHiPs, one of the most successful TV series of the seventies, an equal number will remember me only as a troublemaker; a guy who didn't play by the rules; a loner who never learned the first rule of the entertainment industry: You scratch my back, I scratch yours. My reputation for being difficult began to take root in that skirmish with MGM and Jack Fields. And once the roots took hold, there was just no way to uproot it. And it was only a matter of time before it would reach high enough to strangle me.

I think I could have handled my career moves with more emotional stability, and taken on my enemies without taking in the anger and resentment, if it hadn't been for still another situation that in the months following my accident had spun completely out of control. The combination of stress, fear, and uncertainty that is the inevitable result of almost dying, combined with the daily battle

I was fighting with forces so much bigger and more powerful than I was—including the agency and the studio—would have been enough to tax the resources of anyone. But I had compounded the complexity of my life, and painted myself into a tight little circle, by falling for one of the oldest, and most insidious, traps in the book.

That fall began shortly before I returned to the set to continue work on CHiPs. I was out of the hospital, living alone in a strange apartment and struggling with bouts of depression and self-doubt. Was any of this really worth it anymore? What was I putting myself through, and why? Those were some of the questions I would ask myself over and over. The one that returned every time I shut my eyes and tried to sleep was "Who am I?" Was I still Henry Estrada, that brash young kid from the projects? Or was I Erik, some kind of modern-day matinee idol, a product of the Hollywood fantasy factory? Or had I become Ponch, a character in a TV show, with no real life of his own? I wasn't sure anymore and it was the not knowing that scared me more than anything.

But if I didn't know who I was, then who did? I was feeling the lack of someone in my life whom I could love and trust, a lack that no amount of money or adulation was going to fill. My mother and family all looked to me to provide and protect. But who could I turn to? Who could look in my eyes and say, "I know who you are and you're safe with me"?

It was a sadness made even worse by the powerful painkillers that had been prescribed for me while my body slowly mended. Days at a time would pass when I felt nothing at all but a dull ache in my heart. When that ache finally went away, it was only to be replaced by something much worse—a panic and desperation that no pill could cure.

My mother, who had stayed behind to take care of me, could see the black hole I was diving into, though neither one of us knew where the bottom might be. She, along with my friend Bill Tarman, decided that I had to get out of that tailspin immediately and encouraged me to get away from grim reality for a few weeks and give myself a real chance to recover.

I thought about their suggestion and it seemed like a good idea. Furthermore, I knew exactly the place that had always represented to me the peace and serenity that I so badly needed now: Hawaii. So I packed a few belongings and headed west over the sparkling blue Pacific, bringing my mother and Bill with me for company, along with a registered nurse to monitor my physical well-being. I'd lost a lot of weight since the accident, and although I was eating as much as I could, I wasn't gaining it back. In retrospect, it seems pretty obvious to me what was happening. My body couldn't heal until my spirit healed.

Hawaii was everything I remembered. It had warm sun, lush tropical gardens, and a gracious style of living that took no account of time. We checked into the Kahala Hilton, one of my favorite hotels on the island, and I tried my best to lie back and soak up the soothing aura around me.

But it wasn't easy. A restlessness had gripped me, that feeling of being alone had followed me across the ocean. I needed someone who could understand and sympathize and make the effort to bring me back to a real world that seemed to have faded farther and farther away ever since I saw the front of that car looming up before me.

That was pretty much my state of mind, drugged-out and despondent, when I met Joyce Miller in the hotel lobby. It was nothing more than a chance encounter, really. Considering the foggy state I was walking around in, it's no surprise that I can't really remember the exact circumstances. Maybe she was a fan, maybe she just walked up and introduced herself, or maybe I had given a nod and a wink to this striking woman. All I know for sure is that Joyce Miller was suddenly in my life, and right at the center of my world.

That meeting at the hotel led to a few casual conversations as we crossed paths over the next few days. When it was time to return to Los Angeles, I made a point of seeking her out and asking for her L.A. phone number. When I got back to California, she was among the first people I called. There was something about her, a well-bred air, a sense of self-assurance and good breeding, that drew me irresistibly. Joyce seemed to have it all together, something I needed desperately for myself. Somewhere in the back of my addled brain, I was hoping she could help me.

We dated a few times, turned heads in some tony Beverly Hills watering holes, and ducked into cozy after-hours clubs for long heart-to-heart talks. She told me all about herself, and the story perfectly fit my image of her. Distantly related to the famous Rothschild family, she had been born and raised in Beverly Hills with all the privileges that come with hereditary wealth and position.

A visit to her parents' ivy-covered estate confirmed the impression that Joyce was indeed a class act. All her father ever seemed to do was play golf at the country club, and her mother sat around in a state of royal splendor on Louis XIV furniture, sipping from a sterling-silver tea service. It was all calculated to impress. But then again, everything about Joyce was calculated and she had gauged exactly the effect she was having on a confused veteran of the tough streets of New York. Sure, I'd been traveling in some pretty fast circles since I'd gotten to be a big deal on *CHiPs*, but there always seemed to be a tacky shine to those Hollywood big bucks and all the garish toys they could buy.

Joyce, on the other hand, seemed to travel in a whole different world—one of culture and Old World refinement.

It hadn't been much more than a month of hot and heavy dating when I asked Joyce to move in with me.

"Oh, Erik," she said, "I couldn't do that. I have my good name to think of."

"Of course," I thought to myself. "How could I be so crude?"

Having Joyce around made me feel good about myself again, like I was really worth something. After all, if a twenty-four-carat lady like her was giving me the time of day, that must mean I was better than I felt inside, that I had value. That wasn't what the little voice kept asking me, though, as it chattered away in the back of my brain. Did I love her, or even like her? Maybe in the beginning I did, but it wasn't long before I was unable to separate Joyce from the lavish lifestyle she represented.

Well, if Joyce wouldn't live with me, I had to take serious action to make sure she stuck around to prop up my fragile ego. I asked her to marry me, and while a warning bell should have gone off when I saw how eagerly she accepted, I was in no condition to listen to warnings. I wanted what I wanted, and that was Joyce and the prestigious trappings that came with her.

You could also say that maybe my suspicions should have been aroused when she took me up on my plea to fly to Las Vegas that very night to tie the knot. If she was so concerned about her family, why not hold out for a full-court ceremony, in the grand ballroom of some Rothschild castle in the Bavarian Alps? Instead, what she got was a quickie ceremony at a roadside chapel on the outskirts of Vegas. We were back in L.A. the same day. Within a week I was back at work, feeling as if my life, at last, had gotten on the right track.

It was on track, all right—straight toward the biggest train wreck of my life. When I look back on that period, I sometimes want to find a way to punish myself for being so blind, to take on all the guilt and shame that come with willingly walking into a disaster. It's in those moments that I find it hard to forgive myself, to re-member the condition I was in and how badly I needed a human touch in my life, even if it was the cold-blooded grasp of a practiced and professional gold digger.

Because that's exactly what Joyce was. It was plain to anyone who wasn't in the middle of her web. It was only later that I found out that while I was strutting around the set, bragging to everyone about my rich wife and her gilt-edged family tree, the cast and crew were either afraid to tell me the blunt truth or were just plain laughing behind my back. To them, Joyce was about as genuine as a three-dollar bill, which, it turned out, was about how much money she had in her Gucci purse at any one time.

As word spread about Joyce, Larry Wilcox, who was already jealous of my status on the show and with our audience, became completely unhinged by the thought that I had married into fabulous wealth and a European bloodline. It was just more than he could stand and he let me know in no uncertain terms one day on the set.

"Why don't you just go home and play with your yacht and airplanes and fancy cars and stop driving everyone crazy with your big-shot boasting!" he yelled at me in front of everyone. Honestly, I had to smile. I always got a kick out of getting under Larry's skin.

The press, of course, had a field day when the news of our marriage leaked, playing up the Rothschild angle for all it was worth. I'm surprised, looking back, that some enterprising young journalist didn't dig a little deeper to discover the truth about Joyce. I guess the story she handed me, and I handed everyone else, was simply too good to pass up. We did make a very photogenic couple as the bronzed Latin TV star and his high-brow bride wrapped in furs and glittering with diamonds.

Actually, they weren't exactly diamonds. I don't know how or when the suspicion that Joyce wasn't who she claimed to be finally crept up on me. I think as I started to recover physically, getting back into the swing of work and at last being able to ween myself away from those painkillers, the thick mist that I had been living in began to part. Joyce, for all the supposed fortune she had inherited, always seemed willing and even anxious to let me foot the bill, whether for an expensive meal or a shopping spree on Rodeo Drive. At first I didn't mind, but as the weeks went on I began to wonder where she had stashed her riches.

That germ of skepticism quickly grew into a full-blown hunch that I was being taken, and by a real pro. But I never could find the courage to simply confront her with my doubts. After all, I was the one who insisted that we get married. I felt I would have been almost more embarrassed to uncover the truth than to admit I'd been duped.

But I couldn't quell the sick feeling in the pit of my stomach. I had to know if my new wife was for real, and when I finally got the opportunity, I grabbed it. Joyce was always flashing a diamond ring on her finger the size of an apricot, claiming it was a family heirloom gem that, itself, would have brought in a small fortune. I bided my time and one night, while she was in the shower, snatched the ring off the bathroom counter and hurried into the bedroom.

One swipe of that stone across the dressing mirror confirmed my worst fears. Not a scratch. The rock was about as real as Joyce's pedigree. She was a fake, a pathological liar.

When I started to put it all together, I had to admit that she had really pulled out all the stops to snare me. Maybe she knew about the fifty thousand dollars per episode I had negotiated for CHiPs from the moment we first crossed paths in the Kahala Hilton. "How?" was all I could say. "How did you get those fancy cars that you drove up in for our dates? And those elegant people you introduced to me as your parents at that Beverly Hills mansion. What was their story?"

I never got answers to those questions, but I can't say I really cared all that much either. Maybe she just borrowed everything from friends. Maybe it was all just an elaborate con that she pulled on hapless suckers like me. All I knew was that I wanted to get Joyce out of my life, as quickly and completely as possible.

That, it turned out, was going to be a whole new nightmare.

Chapter Thirteen

I t had been nine months since my accident. Seven months since we had eloped to Vegas. Joyce was now gearing up to get her money's worth for all the hard work she had put into conning me.

I've got to admit, she played the game like a master. Her first move was to set up the proper circus atmosphere for the divorce, turning a healthy profit in the process by selling a bunch of lurid lies to the tabloids.

Fame is great, but like most other great things, it can be abused, and sometimes the abuse is a form of torture so painful you never really recover. People either love you or hate you and the intensity of both those emotions can be overpowering. Anybody who's famous can tell you that there are times when they'd trade all that celebrity status for a little privacy and just a shred of dignity. That's the price most stars have to pay sooner or later, and it's no bargain.

Imagine you're in your friendly neighborhood supermarket, standing in the checkout line with your milk, eggs, and bread. There, in the wire rack by the register, you see your own face on the four-color cover of a weekly rag. Maybe you're mortified. Maybe you're secretly pleased. You pick it up to get a closer look at what they're saying about you. You open the magazine, flipping past pinups in skimpy bikinis and stories about Siamese twins getting married and Marilyn's secret affair with some Kennedy, and then you find your article. Your eyes scan the page as words pop out of the text: "Sexual abuse," "wife beater," "out of control," "violent outbursts," "drug use."

Is that you they're talking about? Panic starts to rise in your throat. How can lies like that be printed with no one even bothering to find out the truth? What can you do to set the record straight? Who can you turn to with your side of the story? Who can you sue? Anyone with any celebrity status will almost certainly face this same scenario sooner or later. And the lies they'll read about themselves may actually have some grain of truth at their core.

I doubt that there are too many stars, yesterday, today, or tomorrow, who have had to endure the kind of orchestrated smear campaign that Joyce Miller put me through. It was ugly, infuriating, and destructive to everything I stood for and had tried to build in my career and in my life.

Over the weeks leading up to our divorce, every tabloid in the country seemed intent on tearing me to pieces on the sharp edges of her vindictive lies. Whatever they paid her for those stories, in my eyes it will always be the same as paying a killer to snuff out a life. Maybe I didn't die, but my reputation and good name suffered a slow and agonizing demise.

There was, according to Joyce, nothing I wasn't capable of doing. I beat her on a regular basis, laying into her, fists flying, on the slightest pretext. I stuck a gun into her mouth, the hammer pulled back, just for the sadistic pleasure of watching her squirm. I forced her to take drugs with me.

I could say that it was all made up, each and every detail, down to the last crossed t and dotted i, but I got tired of defending myself a long time ago. One of the grim truths of fame is that people have an easier time believing the worst about you than they ever do believing the best. One minute you're a hero and the next you're a walking, talking pile of garbage.

I admit I have a temper. I admit there was a time when I did what used to be called "recreational drugs." I even admit that there were times, especially after we split up, that I wanted to do to Joyce everything she claimed I had done.

But I didn't. And I wouldn't. Maybe I was raised in the macho code of the Puerto Rican slums, where it's mano a mano and the one who wins is the one who's still standing in the end. Part of that code, a part that my mother made sure I learned and learned well, was a respect for women. I was furious with Joyce, but I never once threatened or hurt her.

Of course, I couldn't try telling that to a pack of ravenous news-hounds who were only interested in having me for lunch. The sto-ries were so vicious, and spread so quickly, that denial was out of the question. It would only worsen matters. As much as I wanted to defend myself against her horrific accusations, the only thing left was to hope that if I ignored the firestorm building around me, it would eventually burn itself out.

The slander that Joyce subjected me to was like a snowball that, once it got rolling, grew bigger and bigger until it simply ran over me and my life. I've had to carry the wounds of the collision around with me ever since; the shame of people thinking I was a wife beater, or worse, and the simmering rage that comes from not being able to defend myself. Today, I believe that as much as people remember me for my acting, they remember me in connection with the scandal of my divorce. That saddens and angers me, and those are powerful emotions that I've had to learn to live with.

And I have. Which, in the end, I think proves my point. I haven't lost control now and I didn't lose control then. No question about it: I'm an emotional man and I feel those emotions deeply. But I would never, ever inflict my own pain or anger on another human being through physical violence. That's a standard I've held myself to my whole life, beginning with the gangs of Harlem, and as a role model for kids across the country, I feel it's even more important never to lose control.

The same is true of drugs. I'd seen what drugs did to my father and my Uncle Pete and dozens of other guys who spent their days hanging out in the shadows of the projects, waiting for their connection, a fistful of crumpled bills in their dirty hands. I might have snorted a line of cocaine on the set or at Studio 54; I might have smoked a joint with a beautiful and willing starlet who just needed a little coaxing; but I had strict rules when it came to how much and how often. Nothing was going to get hold of me the way it had gotten hold of my father.

Today I regret the fact that I took experimenting with drugs even that far, but not because it gave Joyce more ammunition for her tabloid war. I never forced anything on her. I'm just sorry that I might have set a bad example to the people around me. Even though I might be running a risk by admitting what was just a fact of Hollywood life back then, I want the kids who face today's hard choices to know on which side I stand: Don't play with matches and you won't get burned.

I'm not sure how the unfolding scandal affected *CHiPs* because, even in the middle of Joyce's worst mudslinging, our ratings held steady. Maybe people just liked Ponch, or maybe they wanted to get a good look at the wife-beating drug fiend. Whatever the reason, *CHiPs* constantly won its time slot throughout our third season.

It wasn't the show that was in trouble, it was me . . . The Money. I was going through a very nasty, and very public, divorce; the executives at MGM TV had me pegged as a troublemaker and my agent hated my guts. I was beginning to understand what people

Ed McMahon and I on the set of *CHiPs*

Striking the Ponch pose in a *CHiPs* publicity still

Holding my own in 1987

My *padrino*, Roger Fonesca, and I in 1992

With my boys, Brandon and Anthony, on my *CHiPs* motorcycle in 1993

A photo opportunity on vacation
in Austria in 1993

Larry Wilcox and I in 1992, still
friends through thick and thin

My fiancée, Nanette Mirkovich, and I in 1992

Nanette and I at the International Television Festival in Nice, France, in 1996

Itati Cantoral and Laura Leon (*on my right*), two of my co-stars in *Two Women, One Road*, with me, my mother, and Cuban talk-show host Cristina Saralegui in 1993

Nanette, I, Brandon, and Anthony at home in 1996
Photograph by Maureen Donaldson

meant when they told me that I might have won the battle, but I was losing the war . . . big time.

But I still had friends . . . people who cared about me and showed their concern by doing everything they could to help.

One of them, one of the best, was Bill Young, the car wrangler on *CHiPs*, who was part of a small circle of friends I maintained around the set. That group also included Mike Bondelli, whom I had hired as my stand-in. They were guys who proved themselves ready to stand by me in the worst of times. It was Bill who did more than just lend his support and encouragement. He went out of his way to make the situation better.

"Listen, Erik," he told me, pulling me aside one day between takes, "I'll be honest with you. Your publicity stinks."

"Tell me about it," I glumly replied.

"We've got to do something to clean up your image," Bill continued.

"Look," I said, "I appreciate the concern, I really do. But right now, just being around me is trouble and I wouldn't want any of that rubbing off on you. You'd better just keep your distance."

His answer was to throw his arm around my shoulder. "You know I love you," he said. "We're buddies. You've treated me good, Erik, and now I want to do something to help you if I can."

"What did you have in mind?" was my question.

"Look," he said, "I happen to know someone who's going through a divorce, too. Maybe it's not quite as messy as yours, but she's still feeling it. She could use some company. A few laughs. Nothing serious, just something to take her mind off her troubles. And I think you two would make a great couple."

"Who is it?" I asked, leery of being hooked in to what amounted to a blind date.

"Ever heard of Beverly Sassoon?" he responded.

"Of course," I said. Everyone knew the gorgeous wife of superstar hairstylist Vidal Sassoon. "And it's funny you should mention her.

I happened to see her on a morning show a while ago. She seemed really nice."

"She's gorgeous, too," said Bill with a smile.

"Yeah," I smiled back. "I noticed."

"So," Bill continued insistently. "You want me to give her a call?"

"I don't know" was my answer. "Maybe it's not such a good idea to be dating someone while this divorce thing is going on. Besides, I wouldn't want to drag her into it any more than I would you."

"Don't worry," said Bill. "Beverly can take care of herself. And, like I said, I think you guys would be good for each other."

I heard them calling out for The Money on the set and turned to leave.

"What could it hurt?" said Bill. "A date with a beautiful woman. That's not exactly a hardship, pal."

"Sure," I said. "I'd love to meet her."

That is one decision I have never regretted. Beverly Sassoon turned out to be one of the truest, most genuine, and just plain good people that I ever met. Through all the ups and downs that were to come, she remained a friend, a true friend, and that is harder to find in Hollywood than a real New York pastrami sandwich.

At the time Bill arranged for our first date, Beverly was in the midst of her own private hell, separating from her husband. She had met Vidal while she was a struggling actress, fresh out of Burbank, going by the name Beverly Adams. Vidal was captivated, as was everyone who would meet her, by Beverly's stunning good looks. He made her his primary model for the revolutionary sculpted Sassoon haircut that established his international fame.

While I never got too personal about the reason for their split, I could tell right away that the whole thing was dragging her down. For one thing, she was drinking heavily and continued to battle with alcohol off and on throughout our entire relationship. But she was never too caught up in her own problems to reach out and offer concern and companionship in the midst of my own strife.

We spent a lot of time together after that first night, and I think I knew pretty early on that Beverly and I weren't destined to be husband and wife. For one thing, after my accident I had resolved that I would start a family, and I wanted to soon. Beverly, who already had children with Vidal, didn't want any more. There was no way I was going to change her mind, and I didn't want to.

Having Beverly as a friend was more important to me than having one more romantic fling, even though I couldn't think of a person I'd rather have one with. We were just two people weathering the storms of life, who happened to find a safe haven in each other's company.

Naturally, as my divorce continued to grab the front pages, I found myself seeking out her companionship more and more. We went to A-list parties, premieres, concerts, anywhere and every-where that we could forget our problems for a few hours and bask in a limelight that, for a change, didn't glare like the harsh glow of press interrogation. We were a beautiful couple, trying to find some-thing beautiful in our lives again. It was that connection we had that people respected and maybe even admired.

Most people, that is. As I had feared, as soon as Joyce got wind of my relationship with Beverly, she did her best to turn it to her advantage in the courtroom. She accused me of wasting the money that should be going to her settlement on expensive gifts for my new girlfriend. She had landed a lawyer who justified the stereotype of a lawyer as a cold-blooded shark. It was apparent that this guy was going to turn this case into his own sideshow.

Meanwhile, she kept up the steady drumbeat of negative stories in the press. She even stooped so low as to reveal details of my problems with Larry Wilcox, an ongoing situation that an army of studio publicists had been working on full-time to keep under wraps. I'm sure her revelations about our feuding didn't do much to im-prove my already strained relations with MGM TV.

The showdown finally came in the divorce hearings, when Joyce held back nothing in a display of sheer nerve that even I was stunned to see. When I came to court that morning, there was Joyce in dark glasses, groping for a seat. She was actually pretending to be blind and they had to postpone the whole thing.

By the next court date, she and her lawyer were all business, laying down what they wanted to the last penny. As it turned out, she wasn't entitled to all that much, since we'd been married only seven months. I guess I could have fought her demand for a settlement of $150,000 and a three-year lease on a Mercedes 350 SL. Her lawyer tried to stick me with an additional $30,000 for his fees, but by that time the judge was fed up with both of them and awarded the lawyer only $1,500.

As far as I was concerned, I'd gotten off cheap. One-hundred-and-fifty grand was three episodes of CHiPs and I could pay for the Mercedes lease with the spare change in my pockets. It seemed like a small price to pay to have the nightmare I'd walked right into finally go away. But, of course, it didn't really go away, and the stench of that scandal would dog me from that day on.

All I could do was try to make the best of it and try to put back together the tatters of my career and my life. I decided that after everything I'd been through and as hard as I'd been working, I deserved to take a little time off to enjoy the fruits of all that labor. After we wrapped the third season, Beverly and I took a grand tour of Europe. She was the perfect traveling companion, ready and willing for a night on the town, but just as agreeable to hanging out and relaxing in the hotel room. We really had a good thing going: no pressure, no demands, just the pleasure of each other's company. We'd been over some pretty rough roads together. For a few months it was fun just to pretend that we didn't have any responsibilities, nothing to tie us down.

*   *   *

Then again, there was a part of me that really needed an anchor, something real to hang on to after all the unreality that had turned my world upside down. So, when we got back to the States I moved out of the apartment where I had been little more than camping out since my accident, and bought a real house in Studio City.

It was a spacious spread on a hilltop overlooking the whole valley and the peaks of the San Gabriel Mountains beyond. As soon as I stood on the front porch and took in that panoramic view, I knew I'd found a home.

Standing there, I could see every street I'd lived on since I'd moved to Los Angeles, starting way back at Club California. I remembered the times I'd looked up at those same hills and promised myself that one day I'd be up there, looking down. That day had arrived, and in one of the few moments I'd had to breathe since the whole crazy ride began, I was able to truly savor my success.

It was a success that by then had become so solid that not even the flood of bad press could shake our audience share. *CHiPs* rolled into its fourth season in 1981, as effortlessly as Larry and I drove those big Kawasakis that ate up the asphalt on those endless miles of L.A. freeway. By then, starring in the show was as routine as clocking in to a factory job, and I could put on the character of Ponch as easily as my CHP uniform.

My private life had become a lot more comfortable as well. I divided my time between my new house—painting, furnishing, and decorating it whenever I got the chance—and Beverly's place in Beverly Hills. By mutual consent, we had agreed not to live together. Our friendship was simply too important to risk losing it over some silly domestic squabble.

Things had finally settled down and I was beginning to think that after the long slide that had begun with my accident, my luck was beginning to change. I should have thought again.

Chapter Fourteen

Maybe my luck really had changed, but because there was something inside me that never really felt comfortable or fulfilled, a lack that went back to my earliest childhood memories of a fatherless household, I had a hard time appreciating the turn my life was taking. I was in sore need of someone to take me aside and say, "Listen, Erik. Sometimes it's not a good idea to try to steal second base when you're already safe at first. Bide your time. . . . See what happens when the next guy gets up to bat."

Most guys, if they had been through what I had, would have sat back and let the dust settle, not gone looking to pick another fight. It was time for me to take a low profile, keep my nose clean, and steer clear of confrontation.

But that wasn't how I learned to get through life. I was always walking around with my fists up, ready to sucker-punch the first guy who got in my way, willing to butt heads with anyone who crossed me, no matter how high and mighty they might be. It didn't help that in most cases I was right. I was just asking for what was fair, for what I had rightfully earned and was due. I had never learned the lesson that, sometimes, being right isn't enough. Sometimes you just have to give up and walk away, saving your strength to fight another day. If someone had been there when I was a kid to teach me patience and tolerance and a simple sense of balance, I might have been spared a lot of the grief that came from doing things my way, regardless of the consequences. In the end, I had to learn those lessons by myself. And that's always the hard way.

At the end of CHiPs's fourth year, the show had enough episodes in the can to qualify for syndication and MGM TV wasted no time in announcing the show was up for sale. Syndication didn't necessarily mean CHiPs was on the verge of getting canceled. Most successful shows can sustain audiences both in their first run and in syndication, and CHiPs had proven its popularity over the long haul.

For me, the news that CHiPs was being offered in syndication was nothing but good. I had made it my business to read the fine print of every contract I ever signed, and the one between me and MGM TV was clear as crystal: I had a 25 percent net participation agreement for anything related to the show. In plain and simple language, that meant that if the studio or the network made a dollar from CHiPs, I was entitled to a quarter.

It was a sweet deal, but actually not all that unusual for a star who drives a show's popularity. I knew, for example, that James Garner had the same sort of clause in his contract for *The Rockford Files*, and it seemed only fair because there would be no *Rockford Files* without Garner, and there would be no CHiPs without Estrada. In fact, my stake in the show increased as time went on. In my first year with CHiPs my net participation deal was for around 7 percent. The next year it went up to 14 percent and every year after that I'd grab a couple more points. After four years, I had a nice little nest egg squirreled away with those points, one that could amount to millions of dollars when I cashed them in.

And I was ready to cash them in. When the deal was announced in the trade papers that MGM TV had scored seventy-five million dollars from Golden West Broadcasters, which was Gene Autry's string of independent stations, I knew that, by contract, I was entitled to a chunk of that money. Even though I was collecting on the net and not the gross, I knew I could expect upwards of a cool ten million dollars.

But I also knew something else, which was that most actors who make net participation deals never see a dime of the money promised to them. Of all the fancy footwork that goes on in Hollywood, the fanciest is the fast and loose manner in which bookkeeping is handled. Ask anyone who has ever tried to collect on the back end of some studio deal how much they made, whether it was for writing, acting, or producing. If they don't flat-out tell you they were cheated, they sure will drop a lot of hints.

Well, I'll come right out and say it. Most studios keep two sets of books, one that shows how much they're really making and the other to show how much they're losing. The second set is the one they always trot out when someone comes knocking on the door with their hand out for the money they were guaranteed in black and white. I had heard stories about how Fess Parker had been cheated out of his deal when *Daniel Boone* went to syndication. Even Robert Blake, who owned a third of *Baretta*, never saw dollar one from the sale of his hit show.

I wasn't going to let that happen if I could possibly help it. The day after the news of the syndication sale broke, I called my lawyers, Harry Sloan and Larry Cuppin. They also handled such rising TV stars as Gary Coleman from *Diff'rent Strokes* and John Schneider from *The Dukes Of Hazzard*. I told them to meet me at the offices of David Begelman, the head of MGM. I'd set up a meeting to take place after I had finished the day's shooting.

Begelman's offices were in the Thalberg Building on the old MGM lot and I didn't even have a chance to change out of my uniform before my appointment, so I showed up in full *CHiPs* regalia, including my service revolver.

"I hope you've got real bullets in that gun" was Begelman's opening remark to me. "Because you're going to need them in here."

Then he laughed, trying to signal that it was all in good fun, but I was familiar with the old streetfighting tactic that the best defense is a good offense.

He gestured for us all to sit down, and by that time, after being momentarily thrown by his remarks, I was back on track. "I hear CHiPs is going to Golden West for seventy-five million for a ten-year syndication run," I said. "Congratulations."

Begelman nodded; his face gave away nothing. That guy was cagey.

"I'm happy for you guys," I continued. "And I'm happy for me. I brought my lawyers down here today so we can work out arrangements for payment of my net participation points. Maybe the best way to go about this is in quarterly installments, Mr. Begelman. Would that be acceptable to MGM?" I was all sweetness and light, reasonable and polite to a fault. All the while I was trying to judge the effect my words were having by looking into the hooded eyes of the network executive on the far side of his wide desk.

Begelman stared back at me, unblinking. "Look," he said, his voice low but with a distinct tone of menace lurking in the words, "you've got to wait for the show to be in syndication for a while. See how it does. Then maybe we can talk—"

"Excuse me, Mr. Begelman," I interrupted. "But we all already know how it did in syndication. It did seventy-five million dollars. I read it in the trades."

Suddenly, all the air seemed to be sucked out of the room, as Begelman's face got red and mottled and he stood up, kicking back his chair. "Listen, you spic box boy," he said, spit spraying from his mouth, "why don't you get the hell out of my office and wait in line with every other actor who thinks they've got money coming to them?"

I knew that was a long line. Every actor who had ever taken a television job had hopes of living off the syndication residuals, and most of them had been bitterly disappointed. But that wasn't exactly what I was thinking at that moment. As I felt my temper rise like mercury in a thermometer during a heat wave, another thought, sad and funny at the same time, unspooled in my mind. "I've sold snow cones," I thought. "I've run a Laundromat. I've swept parking lots, cleaned toilets, and been a bouncer in a biker bar. But I've never boxed groceries. . . ."

The room was deathly silent. You could hear the traffic passing by on the street outside and phones ringing in offices down the hall. I turned to my lawyers, who seemed to be interested only in making themselves as inconspicuous as possible. I'm sure if they could have crawled under their chairs, they would have. One of their star clients was actually going toe to toe with one of the most powerful men in Hollywood. That's a scenario no lawyer can think about for too long without getting a migraine.

The ironic thing is that those same two slick lawyers, Sloan and Cuppin, went on to buy a controlling interest in New World Pictures and, years later, had the nerve to call me up and offer me a part in one of their movies . . . at scale. "Hey, guys," I felt like saying, "if you'd gone to bat for me that day in Begelman's office, the measly scale you're offering me wouldn't have amounted to one tenth of one percent of what I'd be paying you just to handle all the money I was due." But I didn't, if for no other reason than that I'd finally learned the value of watching what you say, and who you say it to.

In that moment, however, even if I'd known what to say, I don't think I could have gotten my mouth to form the words. Here was a wheeling, dealing mover and shaker in the entertainment big leagues, dressing me down in the most offensive and demeaning terms he could think of. I always tried to show respect for the professionals I had to work with, even if I didn't feel they really deserved it. Now I was being cut off at the knees by a guy whose fat paycheck I helped to pay for every week.

"Excuse me?" was all I could think of to say, once I got my breath back. "Maybe you should—"

Begelman waved me away with an exasperated gesture. "No," he said. "We're not having this conversation. Get out of my office. Now." And he sat back down and pretended to read some papers on his desk.

I stood up. My cowering lawyers behind me were no doubt hoping the nightmare would end soon. So that was how it was going to be. Well, I could play that game, too. I'd been playing it all my life.

"Okay, Mr. Begelman," I said softly. "I'm leaving. And tomorrow morning you can find yourself a new spic to star in your show."

So there I was again, on the outside looking in, branded as a bad boy, the guy who wouldn't play nice, the fly in the rich, creamy ointment of Hollywood. Looking back, I guess you could say I stepped out of line by asking for what was rightfully mine. I guess you could say that there's no percentage in taking on the big guys, that I should have counted myself lucky, stepped back and been happy for whatever they threw my way.

And, you know what? Maybe you'd be right. By asking for all that money, I'd been taking a risk, a risk that the people I worked for would honor their commitments, a risk that I'd be treated as honorably as I'd treated them, a risk that there is fairness and justice in the world, even if the part of the world you happen to find your-self in is called Hollywood, U.S.A.

Right or wrong, I took that risk. And when I lost, I had to pay the price. As with taking on MGM TV and Jack Fields to get the salary I deserved, I didn't really understand what the costs of self-respect were until it was too late.

Begelman, with the full weight of MGM behind him, was quick to point out just what those losses would be. When I made good on my promise not to show up for work, once again I had to live with the anger and indignity of seeing my name plastered in the head-lines. Once again, I had to endure the unfair accusations that I was a spoiled star, an ego-inflated kid who just wanted to take all his marbles and go home.

But it didn't stop there. Within weeks of that showdown, I got news from my lawyers that MGM had slapped me with a forty-million-dollar breach-of-contract suit. I had to laugh. The suit was proof to me that I was right in claiming that participation money and that the only way they could respond was to throw up a lot of smoke and try to scare me away.

But I wasn't laughing when I found out their next move. An ad in the trades announced an open audition for my replacement in the role of Poncharello. Never mind the fact that I had created that character from the ground up. Never mind that you might as well have tried to replace Henry Winkler as The Fonz or John Travolta as Barbarino. What really hurt me more than anything else was when they started sending me fan letters that said things like "My son could do a better job than that money-grubbing so-and-so. I've enclosed my boy's eight by ten for your consideration."

All I could do was lie back and watch what played out. Half the episodes for the fourth season had yet to be shot, and the plain truth was, CHiPs was the network's only real success story.

I'll never forget, several years later, attending a Golden Eagle Awards banquet honoring Brandon Tartikoff, who had taken the helm at NBC. When he got up to the podium to make his speech, he made a point to single me out of the crowd. "You know," he said, "when I got to this network the only show that still had the lights on was CHiPs and that was thanks to Mr. Erik Estrada. I'm very grateful to you, Erik, for keeping this outfit in business for as long as you did."

It was a nice moment, even with the realization that it wasn't going to bring my show back. I've always considered Tartikoff a real gentleman for making a gesture like that at a time when Erik Estrada wasn't exactly a name people wanted to be associated with.

And the reason for that, of course, was the carefully orchestrated smear campaign launched by Begelman. Stories about my "outrageous demands" and on-the-set tantrums were turning up regularly. The feeding frenzy in the press was matched by rampant speculation about who would replace me on the show.

Since Ponch was one of the most coveted spots on television, there was certainly no lack of hopeful actors ready to leap into his form-fitting costume, but when the network finally made its replacement announcement, I couldn't help being a little surprised.

Bruce Jenner, the Olympic athlete who had been trying for a few years to break into acting, was named to fill my spot, not as Ponch of course, but as an entirely new character in the show. It struck me as weird. One of the most important dynamics of CHiPs had always been the differences between me and Larry, not just in our characters but in the ethnic makeup of that team. Putting two white guys together seemed nothing more than trying to create a whole different show under the CHiPs banner. I wondered how long it would last.

It lasted seven episodes. No matter how negative a picture they had tried to paint of me, no matter how much excitement they had tried to drum up over a new and improved CHiPs, there was no way they could fool the fans who had been loyal to the show and to the Ponch they knew and loved. The ratings numbers for CHiPs dropped through the floor and it wasn't too long after the fourth season wrapped that I got the first tentative feelers from the MGM legal department, "exploring the possibility" of my returning to the show.

I had no objections. Once again, I had mistaken winning the battle for winning the war. I agreed to come back for a fifth season and even tabled the issue of syndication payments for the time being. The truth was, I was only too relieved to be working again. Those seven weeks without a job had reminded me a little too clearly of the days when landing a walk-on part in a movie was a cause for celebration. Acting is like no other job I know. Most of the time is spent waiting for something to happen and the rest of the time goes to worrying whether it will ever happen again.

But I sure wasn't going to let them know how happy I was to be back in the saddle. Short of getting my 25 percent of the syndication take, I stipulated some really steep conditions for agreeing to re-sign with people who, only days before, had been acting like my sworn enemies.

First of all, of course, they had to drop their breach-of-contract suit. Second, I wanted a salary boost to eighty thousand dollars an episode. Third, they would have to pay me for the seven episodes that Jenner had starred in. Finally, I demanded an even million dollars as a sort of goodwill gesture on their part.

Along with that, I demanded a whole new payment schedule, including a million dollars at the start of the sixth season, a million and a half dollars halfway through the season, two million dollars at the beginning of the seventh season and, for good measure, another two million at the end.

They agreed to it all and *CHiPs* was suddenly back in the ratings game. I found it hard not to crow about my victory over Begelman and his cronies. I would have been a lot less cocky if I'd known how close the chickens were to coming home to roost.

Chapter Fifteen

I t was over the holiday season in 1982 that Beverly and I finally called it quits. She had been one of the best friends I'd ever had, and even today she holds a special place in my heart. But the time came when we both realized that if we were going to grow, we would have to do it on our own. Maybe it was just that we'd learned to depend on each other a little bit too much. We were overdue to start living for our future, instead of holding on to the link we had forged in the past.

Leaving Beverly wasn't as hard as it might have seemed because I knew that even though we weren't going to be together as a couple, what we shared would never grow cold. We had so many great times together, jumping on a plane at a moment's notice to attend the wedding of Ed McMahon's daughter in New York and never failing to meet on Friday nights after *CHiPs* had wrapped for an intimate dinner at Ma Maison. We loved each other, but I don't think we were destined to be married because I wanted children and she already had them.

My desire for a family had been kindled, in part, by my close relationship with Beverly's son, Elan. He was a very special kid, sensitive and considerate. I always felt that if I ever had a son, I'd want him to have some of the same qualities that this boy had. I must have known that Beverly and I weren't going to be together forever, because I remember once sitting him down and saying, "Elan, if your mother and I don't work out, I want you to know that I still love you and I want very much for you to be a part of my life." He just nodded and looked back at me with those wide, wise eyes until I thought my heart would break.

It wasn't just my relationship with Beverly that was drawing to an end. Although I would go on to do one more season of CHiPs, the sixth year of a program that I'm proud to say helped define an era in television history, I knew CHiPs wouldn't last too much longer. When I signed on for another season, I made sure to get as lucrative a deal as I could squeeze out of Begelman and MGM: another million-dollar bonus and a hefty hike in my weekly salary.

News of the contract spread around town like wildfire and only added to the fast-accumulating reservoir of resentment toward me that had been building up in the halls of Hollywood power. I was, to be blunt, making a fortune, and there were some very important people who wanted very badly to take me down at least a couple of notches.

At the close of the sixth season, in March of 1983, we learned that the show had been canceled. There was a change in the air, a shift in audience tastes. Cop shows of the CHiPs variety, with flawless heroes and clear-cut bad guys, were giving way to a whole other kind of crime programming, the best example of which was Hill Street Blues, with its large ensemble cast and gritty realism. Hill Street Blues was the first big success that Brandon Tartikoff had after he took over the network, and it signaled the end for the kind of television that I had cut my teeth on.

David Begelman was also coming to the last chapter of his checkered career. Already a convicted felon, he had been caught with his hands in the cookie jar one too many times and would later on take his own life. In the end, I felt only sorry for him, a man who had fallen in love with his own power, using people like pieces on a chessboard.

Being cut loose from the grind of shooting a weekly television show freed me up at last to pursue some long-delayed career moves. As part of my deal with MGM I had a package contract that allowed me to produce TV movies.

The first one on my slate was a boxing drama called *Honey Boy,* in which I starred along with Morgan Fairchild. To prepare for the role I hired a stunt coordinator named Ron Stein and a trainer named Steven "Buck" Buckingham, a close friend to this day. We worked out every day, putting together the moves for the seventeen fights that were going into the *Honey Boy* story, and one day, down at the gym, who should walk in but Sylvester Stallone.

Stallone was well on his way to superstardom at the time, having put the first three *Rocky* films into the box-office black, and he must have been feeling pretty cocky just about then. He later caught up with Ron, who had worked with him on some of the *Rocky* boxing sequences.

"Hey, Ron," he said. "You're not telling that kid any of my secrets, are you?"

"C'mon, Sly," said Ron, in the same kidding tone. "You know I wouldn't give away your techniques."

Sly smiled. "Think the kid would like to go a couple rounds with me . . . do a little sparring to see who's got it and who doesn't?"

"Look," Ron told Sly, "he's just an actor pretending to be a boxer. Take it easy, would you?"

When I heard about it later, it occurred to me that Sly was just an actor pretending to be a boxer, too. I've often wondered who would have won that sparring match if I'd agreed to take him on.

Honey Boy did all right in the ratings, but MGM was not about to exercise any more of my TV movie options. As far as the new regime was concerned I was yesterday's news, and regardless of the nice things Brandon might have said about me in public, no one was rushing over to my house with a new series idea.

For that matter, I never got a call from the legal department asking if they could be of service in clearing up my syndication rights problem. They would have been happy to sweep the whole thing under the rug, but I pushed hard and finally got them to settle on almost eight million dollars. The money was to be paid in three-million-dollar chunks at the beginning of each season. I got the first installment at the beginning of our sixth season, but after we were canceled MGM just put an end to our agreement. I could have fought it, but the whole affair had left such a bad taste in my mouth that I couldn't face coming at them again, no matter how much of my money they had.

After finishing *Honey Boy*, I took some time off to recharge my batteries and assess my options. After breaking off with Beverly I took up with a young actress and model named Kathy Showers, who had done a guest spot on *CHiPs*. She had two little girls from a broken marriage. I loved those two kids and treated them like my own, only drawing the line when one of Kathy's aunts suggested that I adopt them and give them my name. That I wasn't ready for.

Kathy was an incredibly beautiful woman, a kind of walking aphrodisiac, and it didn't come as much of a surprise that men flocked around her like panting dogs in heat. One of those drooling canines was none other than O. J. Simpson. After *Honey Boy*, ICM had gotten me a role on a pilot called *K. O. & Kellogg*, about an ex-football player and a former boxer who were teamed as detectives in San Francisco. My co-star was The Juice and we struck up a casual friendship that included long nights at a Hugh Hefner club in L.A. called Touch. I used to take Kathy there to dance, and as soon as O. J. got a look at her, he ignored me totally and began hitting on her.

That was the end of our budding partnership, even if *K. O. & Kellogg* hadn't been passed on by the networks. I couldn't believe the gall of this guy, who was still married to a beautiful woman named Nicole at the time, trying to move in on Kathy and brushing me off like I was nothing more than a fly.

Kathy, as far as I knew, never did give him the time of day, but I don't think it was out of any particular loyalty to me. My guess is she weighed her options and decided that I could do more for her than a retired football star trying to get into acting. She was very ambitious, pursuing her own acting career for all she was worth. My feeling at the time, having just come off a long, intensive period of hard work, was that the last thing I needed was someone who was interested only in being seen at all the best parties and Hollywood watering holes. But while I might have been willing to go along with her agenda for fame, the nail was hammered in the coffin when she was offered a spread as a *Playboy* centerfold.

My response when she excitedly told me the news was simple and straightforward. "No way," I said. "What we have together is special. It's between you and me . . . not the whole world." Not surprisingly, she preferred the whole world. She went on to become Playmate of the Year in 1985 and grab a few roles in some quickie movies, displaying her assets, but by that time I really wasn't paying too much attention.

After all, I had problems of my own to deal with. In the two years after the set of *ChiPs* went dark, I had finally begun to realize the extent to which my career had been damaged by rumors, innuendos, and bad press. I had landed a new agent, Jack Gilardy, and at first I just sat back and waited for the offers to roll in.

But nothing rolled in except bills. I had invested a lot of my *CHiPs* bounty in real estate, including some beach houses up around Ventura, and was still supporting my mother, so I was looking at a significant nut every month. At first I didn't worry. I still had millions and could see no good reason to trim back my lavish lifestyle. But as the months dragged on and the savings slowly dribbled away, I began to wonder when producers and casting directors would remember that one of the biggest television stars of the seventies was back on the market.

What I didn't realize was that they already knew. Jack worked hard for me at ICM, but it seemed that every place he tried—television, film, even personal appearances—people cared less about my fading star status than my lingering reputation as a troublemaker and a headline grabber. I'd been hooked up through ICM on some celebrity tennis events and a few other ways to keep my name and face out there, but the hard fact was, the business just wasn't interested in giving me another chance. After all, there was a whole new generation of hungry actors looking for a break. Remember all those kids trying out for Ponch?

In desperation, Jack began looking outside the United States to foreign film productions. *CHiPs* had been as popular overseas as it had been in the states and it seemed as if most of the bad publicity hadn't traveled across the borders, so I had a better chance of landing work if I was willing to live out of a suitcase for a while.

One of the first films I got was an Italian production called *Light Blast*, followed by one called *A Show of Force*, which also starred Robert Duvall, Andy Garcia, Lou Diamond Phillips, and Amy Irving. It was an amazing true story about a couple of kids who got caught up in international espionage, and the film was going to shoot on location in Puerto Rico, which gave me a chance to return to a place I hadn't seen since that summer vacation when I was a boy.

The island was as green and gorgeous as I remembered it, but the filming of *A Show of Force* really bogged down when the director,

Bruno Barretto, had a heavy on-location romance with Amy Irving, who at the time was in the process of hauling in a king's ransom from her divorce settlement with Steven Spielberg.

I don't know whether Barretto was after her money, the prestige of being with Spielberg's ex-wife, or just plain was head over heels in love with her, but he shifted the whole focus of the film to Amy and the finished product disappeared without a trace at the box office.

I continued doing foreign movies, including one in Thailand and a few more in Italy, but it was obvious that my career was taking a serious dive. I just couldn't shake all the negative connotations that came with my name. Although I suspect that a few phone calls from high places also contributed to my being almost totally blackballed in Hollywood, there's nothing concrete I can point to. All I know is that doors were slamming in my face everywhere I turned, and the reason given more often than not was that I was too much trouble, too temperamental, and just a plain pain in the ass.

I had come to Hollywood to be an actor, but I'd ended up as a television celebrity, and there was a world of difference between the two. One was a craft, the other, in many ways, was a con. I was a pretty face and hard body in a tight uniform, going through the motions every week with no real connection to the art of acting. After all, how many different ways were there to play Poncherello?

I was determined to reconnect with my roots as an actor, and through ICM I got a part in the prestigious Off-Broadway theater, Cherry Lane, in a production of Sam Shepard's play *True West*, playing one of two brothers who confront their fears during a single sweltering night in Los Angeles. It was serious drama, with a character that gave me real room to express myself, and it helped me realize that however far I had gotten from the rewards of acting, they were still there if I would only seek them out.

True West ran for eight sold-out weeks in the summer of 1985, and when the curtain came down on the last performance I felt revitalized. Sure, four hundred dollars a week was a little less than I was used to getting for my services, but there was simply nothing like playing to a live audience every night, performing that exhilarating high-wire act that is live theater. This, I told myself, is what I'd been missing all those years living in a trailer and letting myself be propped up in front of a camera like a stand-up display.

But starring in Off-Broadway productions wasn't going to pay the rent, and before long I was back beating the bushes for a real job. It was the same disheartening grind I'd faced for almost three years, made even worse by the fact that even my *CHiPs* calling card was beginning to look a little frayed and faded. A hit TV show in the seventies was old news in an industry that thrived on what's new, hot, and happening in any given fifteen minutes.

When you're in the loop of that exciting, adrenaline-pumping flurry of popping flashbulbs and adoring crowds, you have to keep reminding yourself that it's not going to last forever. And if you start believing that myth, when the inevitable finally does happen and you're on the outside looking in, it can really twist your head around. It's so hard to understand how you can be the object of so much adoration one day and an almost embarrassing reminder of a bygone era the next.

I can't say I was completely immune to the fantasy of fame. I had been on top for so long, I had a hard time remembering what it was like to struggle and strive to get yourself noticed. When it happened, it was a wrenching adjustment and one that left me very much alone, frustrated, and feeling sorry for myself.

After *True West* I kind of drifted for a while. I went to Monte Carlo to appear in a French commercial for a line of leather jackets and, realizing that I had no good reason to come back, bounced around Europe for the better part of six months. I told myself I wanted to see the sights—Paris, the South of France—but I think what I was really doing was looking for something, some nameless destination where my restless spirit could find peace.

That serenity I was looking for, of course, could be found only inside, but I didn't know that at the time and had to follow my obsessive, driven desire to find the answer in new places and other people. It was that same search that had taken me to the workaholic brink during my years in *CHiPs*, the same empty feeling that had compelled me to propose marriage to Joyce. Whether it was my lifelong search for a missing father, a delayed reaction to the adolescent wish fulfillment that fuels the Hollywood dream, or an emotional and spiritual emptiness that comes with the territory, the effect was a deep longing and desperate hope that tomorrow would not be the same as today.

The truth was, during those months, every day was pretty much the same, and I did whatever it took to avoid that moment of truth when I would finally look inward and honestly evaluate the faults and flaws that got me into so much trouble, both in my career and in my personal life. But that time hadn't yet come, and instead I looked for still another way to escape the dead end I had run blindly into. And that's where Peggy came in. She was one more escape, one more trap, one more mistake that I would end up paying for in bitter tears and helpless rage.

Chapter Sixteen

Like a lot of quick flings and one-night stands, I had met Peggy at a club. It wasn't too long after I'd called it a day with Kathy Showers and I was still very much in the rebound mode. I missed that wild romantic surge that comes in the first few months or years of a relationship, before it starts to cool and the hard work of maintaining a connection begins.

When I look back on that time, I realize that for me love meant eyes meeting across a crowded room, the thrill of the chase, the dizzy sensation that comes with the first kiss. I really didn't know what lay beyond all those romance novel clichés, and even if I had known, whom could I have turned to for the real thing? Women were still sucked into the aura of my fame, faded as it may have been, and I was so used to succumbing to temptation that I had numbed myself to all the emotional cues that led to a true and lasting love.

At the same time, I was blind to the signs that could have warned me against the vampires and parasites and cold, calculated users who prowled the nightlife. If I saw a girl who had the look, and who let me know that I had the look, that was all I ever needed to make a move, or let myself be moved in on.

Peggy had the look, that bronzed, blond California surfer girl aura that radiated sex appeal. It was carefully cultivated to give off just the right combination of availability and aloofness, an attitude that I had seen a thousand times before in a thousand clubs just like that one.

She was originally from Long Beach, just outside Los Angeles, where she worked as a waitress, and the sultry, silky exterior she presented in the club hid a troubled past. She had a record as a delinquent that included a stay at the Sybil Brand Institute, an L.A. County women's detention center, and had developed the hard edge and ruthless cunning of a real streetwise operator. She also had had a child out of wedlock, whom she had put up for adoption. But Peggy was good at hiding parts of her personality and past, dressing up in the guise of a good-time party girl just looking for a little fun.

She was a friend of a friend, and when he introduced us, I liked what I saw. I was still feeling the pain of losing Kathy, and Peggy looked like just the candidate to make the ache go away. Mother's Day was coming up, and I had a tradition of flying my mom out for a little catered celebration with a few close friends and family members. Peggy used her demure smile and the healthy glow of her perfectly proportioned body to play me like a fiddle. I found myself inviting her up to the house for the party.

From that moment on, things fell into place like polished steel tumblers in a bank vault. Peggy took up where Kathy had left off, becoming my constant shadow, live-in lover, and financial responsibility. By the time I had landed the part in *True West* she was a permanent fixture and I didn't think twice about inviting her along with me to stay in New York for the run of the play.

When I came to find out, years later, that Peggy had made a bet with a girlfriend that she would someday marry a star, suddenly a lot of things made sense for the first time. That includes the gleam in her eye the first time we walked into the plush suite of the Helmsley Palace, where I was going to live while in New York, paying the

$225-a-day tab out of my own pocket. It was a lifestyle Peggy could get used to with no problem whatsoever.

She came along with me from New York to Monte Carlo, and on that long, aimless trek through Europe. I had become so used to having someone by my side all the time, someone to chase away the realization that my life was going badly offtrack, that I really didn't give her a second thought. She was just another part of the scenery, one in a long line of beautiful women who wanted a part of me. Love? It never entered the picture, and for that I have only myself to blame. I should have told her right up front how I felt, drawn the line and stood firm. But I guess in one way I was using her as much as she was using me. I needed someone by me, someone who could make me forget for a few hours, or even a few minutes, the gnawing loneliness. And she needed someone with the money and prestige and power to give her what she wanted. I was the designated sucker.

When we finally flew back to L.A., Peggy was in no mood to pick up the reins of her old life of living with her parents in a suburban tract house on the outskirts of Long Beach. I didn't have a problem with her moving into the Studio City house. The place seemed so empty and quiet the first day I got back, the thought of being there alone was more than I could tolerate.

Our mutually convenient connection continued as the weeks turned into months, floating along like driftwood on an ebb tide. I don't know how long I might have stayed with Peggy if things had worked out differently—another week, another month, or as long as it took to find someone I could really care about. For her part, Peggy was careful to keep her true intentions hidden. She played the role of a true-blue friend expertly. She was there for me when I needed her, was willing to go the extra mile, catered to my vanity, and lulled me into thinking there was nothing really wrong with sharing my bed—and my life—with what amounted to a total stranger.

In the end, that's who Peggy was, a stranger, as dangerous and malicious as any home invader who had broken into my house to steal my valuables. Sure, I invited her in, but the person I let through the door wasn't the same person who came to me after almost a year with news that rocked my world. That person was a cunning, calculating opportunist, one who had worked her way into a comfy little scene that she had no intention of letting slip away.

Peggy informed me flatly that she was pregnant, as if daring me to do something about it.

"But I thought you were on the pill," I said, shocked and dismayed.

She shrugged. "Things happen."

"You bet they do," I thought. If the pill was supposed to be 99 percent effective, I wanted to ask, how was it that I got stuck with that last 1 percent? But I kept my suspicions to myself. It didn't seem like the time or place to bring that issue up.

"Look," I said, as gently as I could, "I don't have a steady job and it doesn't look like one's about to turn up. I'm in no position to get married. I'm sorry that this has happened but let's not compound one mistake by making another."

What I should have said was that I didn't love her, that I never had and that I never would, and that any scheme she had that would keep us together, for the sake of a baby or anything else, was wrong for us and would be wrong for the baby. But I didn't. I was scared and I was worried, and I frankly didn't know what to do.

She waved off my feeble objections. "I'm not going to give this baby up," she insisted. "I did that once and it's not going to happen again."

I could hear the stubborn tone in her voice, and in an instant it alerted every instinct I had to fight back. If she was going to dig her heels in, I could dig in even deeper.

"I can't have a kid," I said right back at her. "Maybe one day, but not now." Again, I left unsaid what I should have told her loudly and clearly—"And not with you."

"Fine," she said with a haughty sniff. "Then I'll just go back to France and raise the baby there." Peggy had a sister in France who had married a wealthy restaurateur, and she had once toured the country as part of a dance troupe.

It sounded like a plausible alternative, but it sent a cold chill up my spine. A vivid picture flashed through my mind: a little boy or a little girl, growing up without ever knowing who their father was. "No way," I said. "That's not going to happen. No kid of mine is going to grow up without me around. You can't do that. I won't let you."

"You got any other ideas?" she shot back, with her hands on her hips.

"Let me think," I said. But even then I could feel her claws tightening around my throat.

It wasn't too long after Peggy dropped her bombshell that I finally landed a job in another Italian production, *Il Repentito . . . The Repentant*. All things considered, it was a pretty fitting title at that time in my life. I played a famous Mafia godfather, Michele Greco, and the movie was filmed in Palermo. I took Peggy with me on location, just to keep an eye on her as much as anything else. She was already starting to have morning sickness, and by the time our flight arrived in Rome she was even showing a little.

While we were filming *Il Repentito* I got friendly with an Italian character actor named Salvatore Bila, who had a lovely wife and some great kids of his own that he supported, when he wasn't acting, by delivering seafood to restaurants. He was a good, kind, and caring man, and with no one else to turn to, I took him aside and confided to him my predicament.

In the weeks following Peggy's announcement, I had been giving a lot of thought about the right thing to do and by the time I buttonholed Salvatore, I'd made up my mind. "I've got to get married," I said. "The sooner the better. Can you help me?"

He smiled and slapped me on the back. "Don't worry," he assured me. "Salvatore will take care of everything."

And he did, arranging for a priest and handling all the details for a good Catholic wedding at the Basilica de San Paolo in Rome. I bought Peggy the prettiest wedding dress I could find, and her sister came over from France to be the maid of honor. I was determined to make the best of the situation.

There was only one detail I couldn't take care of. "Mom," I said, over the phone from Rome just before the ceremony, "there's something I need to tell you."

She was furious with me for going ahead with such a major move without consulting her. But more than anything, I think, she was deeply hurt that I would go behind her back that way. She had met Peggy the year before at my Mother's Day party and had gotten the distinct impression that she was just another one of her son's romantic flings.

"Don't do this, Papo," she pleaded. "It isn't right."

"I've got to, Mom," I said, choking back tears. "I've got no choice."

She hung up without another word and for the next three years refused to see me. My sister felt the same way. Suddenly I was cut off from the only real support I'd ever had, my family. I continued to send money to my mother and tried many times to reach out, but my marriage of necessity had put up a barrier between us, and it seemed that nothing could get around it.

My son, Anthony Eric Estrada, was born on March 1, 1986, and from the minute I saw him, I had new hope that maybe, after all, everything would work out right. I insisted on being in the delivery room to cut his umbilical cord. As I held that little squirming bundle in my hands, I felt for the first time in my life as if a big missing piece of a puzzle had finally fallen into place.

I hadn't had the dad I needed when I was growing up. Now I had the chance to be a dad for another little helpless kid and, by doing so, maybe break the chain of loss and loneliness that had always linked me to the past.

I never let Anthony out of my sight for those first few weeks, even though I had hired a wonderful Salvadoran nurse named Teresa to help with the new addition. I wondered, when I held him in my arms and saw the way he stared up at me with complete trust, if maybe we had made the right decision after all. Suddenly having a family, even with a wife who, deep down, I knew wasn't the right woman for me, filled a lot of the empty spaces inside. I had a new-found sense of security that I wanted to hang on to, no matter how flimsy the foundation of our marriage might have been.

Already there were new cracks developing. Right after we had a ceremony naming my dear friend Jimmy Komack, the creator of *Welcome Back, Kotter*, and his wife, Cluny, as Anthony's godparents, a feud developed between me and Peggy as to how the boy would be raised.

Naturally, I wanted him to be brought up in the Catholic Church, like his old man, but Peggy was having none of that. She was intent on sending him to a Protestant school, and all I could do was go along with her. I was so determined to give that little guy every chance I hadn't had that I wasn't going to let my growing alienation from his mother get in the way if I could help it.

Which was why, when Peggy broached the subject of having another baby, I agreed. I didn't think it was healthy for any kid to be an only child. Even if it meant tying myself even more tightly to Peggy, I wanted to do the right thing for my son.

My second son, Brandon Michael Paul Estrada, was born eighteen months later. Holding him in my arms brought up those same tender and protective feelings that I now realized were the best part of being a father. At the same time, I was beginning to crack under the strain of an increasingly tense and troubled homelife.

Before the marriage, holidays were always a time when I gathered my family from both coasts to spend time with me. After that, it was only Peggy's sister or her friends who came by. Around the Thanksgiving dinner table were guests who, as far as I was concerned, might as well have been brought in off the streets. No matter how hard I tried, I couldn't seem to heal the wound I had inflicted on my mother and sister by marrying Peggy. There was more than one time when I found myself alone and crying at the thought that Anthony had never seen his grandmother and that she had never seen her grandchild.

I tried to lose myself in my sons, but it was getting harder and harder to shut out reality. Work had almost completely dried up and I was running through my savings and other assets at an alarming rate. Peggy, meanwhile, seemed to get more and more possessive and jealous with each passing day. It didn't matter what was happening, if she felt excluded or ignored, she did her best to make life miserable for everyone.

She had a real problem with the closeness of my relationship with Anthony and Brandon and even objected when Teresa, the nanny, tried to teach the boys a little Spanish. I thought it was a good idea, a way to connect the kids to their roots, even though I didn't speak the language of my people. But Peggy wouldn't hear of it. It came down to a power play, a battle over who was going to run the house. Because I was so disheartened and demoralized, all I could do was back off and let her have her way.

I was trying everything I could to keep my career from stalling completely, which included once again accepting invitations to celebrity tennis tournaments and other sporting events for charity. I figured, as long as someone still thought I was a celebrity, I might as well go along with the gag. But Peggy would have none of that, either. If the invitation didn't include free airfare and accommodations for wives and children, she insisted that I turn them down.

She had the same inflexible attitude about real work. When I got an offer to do a movie in Peru, she raised hell when she found out she would have to stay behind. Then she went totally ballistic when she read the script and came across a love scene I was going to play. That time, however, I put my foot down, as much for the prospect of being away from her for eight weeks as for the small amount of money the job would generate.

She sensed that her ride was coming to an end. Even though I hadn't said how I really felt, she could see that I was getting more and more depressed and starting to have real trouble even sleeping through the night. As she saw it all slipping away, she tried one last desperate ploy to keep me hanging on. If one kid wasn't going to do it, and two wasn't enough, she'd try for three.

This time I absolutely refused, but saying no to Peggy was like trying to stop an oncoming train by holding up your hand and asking pretty please. She was going to have that kid, if for no other reason than the additional insurance against my leaving it would give her. The only problem was that I'd long since stopped sleeping with her, so if she was going to get pregnant she'd have to pull off a pretty fancy move.

"It's going to be hard to be anonymous again" was the first thing out of her mouth and, to me, that pretty much summed up her stake in our relationship. No matter how far down my career had gone, to her even the fading glow of celebrity was better than being just another citizen on the street. I thought it was pathetic. If I'd had the choice right then, I would have given up everything, all the bright lights and big checks I had once known, just to live a normal happy life.

But of course, my happiness wasn't on Peggy's agenda, and at first she flat-out refused to consider divorce. But as she realized how completely determined I was to try to put my life back together without her, she started a long and tortuous process of bargaining. First, she demanded that we try to patch things up with a marriage counselor. I had no objection. For the first time in years I knew what I was going for, and if this was the only way to get there, then so be it.

From our first session with the counselor, a wonderful and understanding woman with an office in Encino, I tried to make my position as clear and straightforward as possible.

"We're here because we want to fix our marriage" was Peggy's opening remark.

"No we're not," I shot back. "We're here because our marriage is over and we need to work out our divorce in a way that will cause the least pain to ourselves and our children."

That was that, and after four more sessions of basically repeating myself, the counselor could see the handwriting on the wall. She suggested I move out of the house for a trial separation, and the next day I rented a one-bedroom apartment back down in the valley, as close to my house and my kids as I could find.

The next two years of my life, while they were no picnic, at least had an element of hope that had been completely extinguished during my miserable marriage to Peggy. I spent as much time as I could with Anthony and Brandon, driving them to school and picking them up, taking them to movies or the park or just for long walks down Venice Beach. Again, I was determined to be there for them.

Meanwhile, I was doing everything I could to smooth the process of divorce for Peggy. I offered to let her keep the house or, if she chose, to buy a new one. It wasn't exactly as if I could afford to do either. I was virtually tapped out by that time. Peggy wasn't helping by going on endless shopping sprees while she could still rack it up on my credit cards.

When she finally realized that she'd run out of moves and manipulations and agreed to the divorce, I thought, at last, that I was home free. No such luck. Months rolled by as she dragged her feet on every detail of the settlement and made the custody issue a real sticking point. She knew that was the one area where I wouldn't give ground. While she tried to limit me to weekend visitations, I argued for weekday rights as well.

In the end, I got pretty much what I wanted—Tuesdays and Thursdays and every other weekend—if it could be said that anybody really gets what they want in a nasty and contentious divorce case.

The lawyers got exactly what they wanted, a cool ninety thousand dollars, which would have been more than enough for Peggy to move into a brand-new house to start a brand-new life. But Peggy didn't want it that way, and as the case dragged on, I started realizing that I had to fight back with everything I had if I was going to walk away with even the shirt on my back. I withdrew my first offer of letting her have the house, but had to compromise when the judge ruled that she could live there for another year, with me footing all the bills. It was only then, after nearly two years of living in that one-room apartment, that I was able to move back into my place on the hill.

Not that I had all that much to move back to. My family was shattered. I had agreed to pay almost three thousand dollars a month in alimony, which, of course, guaranteed that I was going to be perpetually scrambling to make ends meet. During her stay Peggy seemed to have done her best to utterly destroy the place. The day I walked through the door I was almost knocked down by the acrid scent of cat spray as strays roamed around the place like they owned it.

But the worst of it, by far, was trying to pry my boys away from her for my visitation days. After she'd been thrown out of the house, she shacked up for a while with the lawyer who had handled her case, and every time I came out to his Brentwood house to pick up Anthony and Brandon, she made some kind of scene, shouting and crying and accusing me of deserting my kids. On one nightmarish afternoon, she actually attacked me, kicking and hitting, utterly oblivious to the fact that I had Anthony in my arms and was doing my best to shield him from her insane assault.

Divorce, even if a marriage is dead, is a terrible thing, and the ones who suffer the most are always the children. If they don't feel somehow responsible for the breakup, then they've got to deal with choosing sides between their mom and dad. No kid can handle that kind of pressure, and I could see the effect it was having on Anthony and Brandon. All I could do was let them know, over and over again, that I loved them and that no matter what they would always have a father.

It was a heartbreaking situation and I can't think of a time when I was more emotionally devastated. I would find myself crying for no reason at all, wandering through the empty rooms of my house, trying to remember what it had been like when the world seemed to be laid out before me. I was a star, loved by millions, with hopes and dreams for a happy future. A loving wife, happy children, my mother and family safe and secure under my wings . . . it all seemed like the inevitable Hollywood happy ending. I was going to be the patriarch, like Papa Dompino, a tower of strength, loyal and loving and wise.

But that dream had vanished like the slow fade at the end of a canceled TV series. Now I was Erik Estrada, the has-been, the divorced father of two, broke and unemployable, a joke in the industry and a failure to his family.

* * *

Did I ever think of killing myself, ending it all with the easy way out? No. I clung to life even when my life seemed to be hanging by a thread. I had a responsibility, not just to Anthony and Brandon but to myself. Once I had so much potential, so much promise. It all couldn't have just vanished. It all couldn't have been the foolish hopes of a Puerto Rican kid who loved to see John Garfield, bigger than life, on a Broadway movie screen. There had to be a second act, a new beginning, a chance to start all over again.

For Christmas that year, 1988, I had to borrow money—twenty thousand dollars—from my brother-in-law, Myron, to clean up the house and bring my mother out for the holidays. It was the first time I had been face-to-face with her since I made that fateful phone call from Rome, and the feelings that swelled up as she stepped off the plane seemed to mix pain and pleasure, rejoicing and regret, in one almost unbearable moment.

Here was the woman I had always looked to for strength and guidance and devotion that was completely unconditional. My mother loved me with a love that time or fate could never fade, and now here she was again, there for me, her little Papo. I would always be her son and always find a place in her arms, no matter how far I strayed or how many mistakes I made.

Our reconciliation was the one bright spot during that dark time of my life. Desperate for work to meet my meager living expenses and alimony payments, I would take any job that came my way, including under-the-table non-union productions. It was only a matter of time before the Screen Actors Guild caught wind of my activities, which they claimed were strictly forbidden under union rules.

Well, that wasn't exactly true. I did some research and found right-to-work statutes that allowed any union member to declare himself in need of work, union or otherwise, without fear of penalty or losing his pension or insurance.

I pointed all this out to the disciplinary board of SAG and it had exactly no effect whatsoever. They made it clear that I had to play by their rules or get out of the game. It was the Hollywood shuffle all over again, and if I ever hoped to land another acting job, I knew I'd have to buckle under. That old fighting spirit, the determination to win the battle even at the cost of losing the war, had finally been crushed. I agreed to every humiliating demand they made: paying back in fines the few dollars I'd made working non-union; speaking to young actors at seminars about the dangers of breaking industry regulations; and taking out a letter of apology in *The Hollywood Reporter*.

It wouldn't have done any good to try to explain what I was going through, that I'd been out of work for too long to remember, that I had bills that I couldn't pay, that I needed the chance to act. Hollywood is a tough town that has heard it all before, and SAG had a vested interest in making an example of me, a former television superstar. By that time, I was pretty much getting the hang of being a whipping boy.

Chapter Seventeen

There comes a time in everyone's life, no matter how successful the final outcome, when a person hits bottom. It's the point when everything not only seems to be going wrong, but seems as if it will never go right again; when everyone you turn to turns away from you and everything you touch crumbles in your hand.

The problem is, of course, that you never really know if it's the real bottom that you've touched. Maybe you've still got further to fall. Maybe the ground will open up under your feet and swallow you whole.

It's only in retrospect that I recognize those moments in my life. Only when I look back can I pinpoint the moment when things were at their absolute worst and there really was no place left to go but up.

By the fall of 1990, I had reached that bottom, even though I wasn't sure whether the free fall I'd been on for five years was finally over. It's only when I think back to the day when I saw a tall, shapely woman working out in my neighborhood gym that I can positively say, "Yes, that was it. That was the moment my luck began to change."

Right up until then, my personal life had been about as bleak as my professional prospects. For a while after Peggy left, I took up with Kathy Lautner, my old girlfriend from those early days at CHiPs. But it quickly became evident that, with my divorce and diminished bank accounts, I really wasn't all that much fun to be around. I can't say that I blame Kathy. After all, I was walking around with a thick black cloud over my head night and day.

I continued the habit of exercising regularly at Take Twenty Gym, down the street from my house. I was determined that even if everything else in my life was falling apart, I could at least keep my body in shape.

To me, it was ironic that a guy who was once called a sex symbol had become shy and tongue-tied around a woman, but that's exactly the reaction I had when I saw Nanette doing her circuit on the free weights and StairMaster.

There was something different about her, a warm glow in her long oval face that came from more than the heat of her workout. She wore her hair long and had huge brown eyes and kept her shapely body trim. But what really caught my attention was the way she always seemed to have a smile for everyone. People, I immediately saw, liked her. They liked being around her. She made them feel comfortable and at ease.

It had been too long since I'd felt either comfortable or at ease, with myself or with anyone else. So for the first few weeks I just hung back, watching her exercise and becoming more and more intrigued by this mysterious and charming woman.

When I finally got up the nerve to approach her, I felt like a kid again, like little Henry Estrada asking Margaret O'Boyle to the movies for the first time.

"Hey," I said. "I'm Erik. I've seen you around here a lot."

She laughed, a sound like a wind chime in a breeze. "I know who you are," she said. "I used to get to watch you on TV when I was little . . . if I finished all my homework, that is."

I laughed, as much to cover my bad case of nerves as anything else. "Listen," I said swallowing hard, "I'm a member of the Screen Actors Guild and they're having Academy Award screenings soon. Would you like to go with me?"

She didn't answer me right away, but instead just gave me a long once-over, appraising me in that forthright but not unfriendly way of hers.

"Hey," I said hastily. "It's not really a date or anything. I just need . . . some company. Look, you can consider me gay if that helps."

She laughed again and the wind-chime sound echoed in my ears. "Gay people go to the movies, too," she said. "I'd love to." She stuck out her hand. "My name's Nanette."

Well, we never did go to the movies. It seemed like a complete waste to me to sit in the dark with such a special person, watching celebrities cavort on a flat screen instead of getting to know her. We went out to dinner instead and sat and talked for three hours, way past the start time for the screening. Neither of us noticed.

When I drove Nanette home that night I asked her out again, and she agreed. But over the next few days, I started wondering if the qualities I had seen in her were real or just some last-ditch illusion sprung from my lonely soul. I broke our date, and by the time I found the courage to approach her again, I was sure she had totally written me off.

She hadn't. And she wouldn't. And for the first time in my life I began to understand what the company of a good woman can do for a man, even a man so gun-shy he isn't even sure he can trust himself.

Nanette Mirkovich was one of twelve children in a sprawling English-Croatian clan that had settled in the San Fernando Valley. Her father was a stamp and coin collector and amateur violinist, and her mother managed an unruly brood with a firm but loving hand. Nanette, the youngest of the family's girls, had become the family's designated baker and cook and over the years had learned to create breads and desserts that would humble even a French chef. As she once told me, in a family that large she realized early on that if she wanted to have a cake on her birthday, she was going to have to bake it herself.

Nanette had also inherited her mother's calm and competent skill as a can-do organizer. She had a job running a post-production studio and could handle everything from answering phones to re-pairing a balky VCR.

You could say it was love at first sight, but I don't think I even knew what real love between a man and woman was then. I'd had so many one-night stands and purely sexual attractions in my life that the idea of just being with someone, enjoying their company with no strings attached, was a complete novelty. But I knew something was different about my feelings for Nanette because, this time around, sex was the last thing on my mind. What I wanted more than anything was to be close to her, the way a freezing man wants to get close to a warm fire.

It was the same feeling I had about her family. The closeness they shared, the ease and natural pleasure they took in each other's company, and the love that flowed between them is what I had wanted to be a part of my whole life.

And, even though I was not much more than a stranger to them, they didn't think twice about inviting me into their family circle. That Thanksgiving, I was due to have my boys over to the house and when I told Nanette, she immediately invited all three of us over for a big Mirkovich feast.

I'll never forget that day together, playing chess with her little brothers, laughing at all the silly jokes her father told, and even enjoying old family stories of people and places I knew nothing about. This, I realized, was what a real family was all about, and I was glad that Anthony and Brandon were there to see and share in the love and commitment that were as nourishing as Nanette and her mother's delicious food.

"Do they know who I am?" I asked Nanette later. I was afraid that if they'd ever heard the name Erik Estrada, it was only in connection with one of the sleazy scandals that I'd suffered through.

"Not until you showed up at the door," she replied. "I just told them that I'd met a guy who was divorced and had a couple of kids and that maybe they'd recognize him when they saw him."

"Did they?" I couldn't help but ask.

"Erik," she said. "Relax. They like you . . . and I like you."

"Listen, Nanette," I said as earnestly as I knew how. "You don't have to say anything that you don't mean. I don't want anything from you except to be your friend, to hang out together. I don't know why, but I feel at peace when I'm around you."

"I'd like that," she said, looking straight into me as if she could read what was written in scar tissue on my soul. "We can be friends for as long as you want. I know you've been through a lot, but I want you to know that I'll be here to help in whatever way I can. For as long as you want."

It was hard for me to believe that someone would be saying those words to me, someone who didn't want anything from me, who wasn't interested in my celebrity status or my money or my access to the best parties at the best addresses or the possibility that I might be a stepping-stone to further their career. Nanette liked me for who I was, not for who people thought I was, or who I pretended to be, or even who I hoped to be. Just me. The real me. And for the first time in as long as I could remember, I started to like myself a little better, too. If someone as honest and good and caring as Nanette Mirkovich could find something in me that was worthwhile, some spark of humility and a capacity for love that had come from so much hard experience, then maybe, just maybe, I could begin to accept it myself.

For so long, people had been hammering me with accusations and lies, lawsuits and headlines, and wounding words that cut so deep I had started to believe what they said. Henry Estrada, the kid who set out to conquer the world had long since shriveled and died. In his place was Erik Estrada, a man cut down to size. Suddenly, there was an angel in my life, offering to take me by the hand, to help me stand up straight again. When I cried that night, alone in my house, the tears came from a spring of joy that I thought had dried up a long time ago.

With Nanette in my life, I naturally wanted to do whatever I could to help the process of healing and wholeness along. I was all but bankrupt, but I borrowed twenty thousand dollars to renovate my house, cleaning and painting and rebuilding right alongside the crew of Mexican workers I had hired.

Our relationship continued to grow, slowly but steadily, like a tree taking root in fertile ground. Even when Peggy reared her head again, selling stories of my so-called abusive behavior to the rags and even appearing on television talk shows to grab a few more minutes of notoriety by dragging out all the old lies, it didn't bother me nearly as much. It hurt and I wished that she would simply let the past die as I had, but I can't control what other people do. I can only be responsible for my own actions, to be as good and kind and fair as possible to everyone I meet. And when I'm not sure what to do or say I always ask myself, "How would Nanette handle this?" It works every time.

But it wasn't just a clean house and a clean conscience that were making the difference in rebuilding my life. I also got a clean start in my career. It was as if finding something good and hanging on to it had opened the door for other good things to come, and once

Nanette arrived, a whole new beginning for me followed close behind.

After nearly ten years with ICM, I finally realized that if I was ever going to work again, I'd have to find new managers and agents, people who could look beyond the past and take hold of the future. By then, in early 1991, I hardly had two nickels to rub together and wasn't really sure I even had a future. But I made the leap and signed with an aggressive young management team at the Sterling-Winters Company, who almost immediately got back to me with a job offer.

But there was a catch. The project was in Spanish, and, while I could barely get by with my Puerto Rican Spanglish, I certainly couldn't do justice to the language for a Latin audience. Yet, while I was in Mexico City doing another film in which my voice was dubbed into Spanish, I met with producer Emilio La Rosa. He assured me that my voice could also be dubbed for his production and the results wouldn't be embarrassing to me.

I agreed to take a look at the script. When it arrived, my worst fears were confirmed: Johnny may have been raised in the U.S.A. but he was speaking fluent Spanish on the page. It was way out of the range of anything I could handle.

I was about to call La Rosa and tell him the deal was off, when something stopped me. Maybe I'd look like a fool trying to speak Spanish. But fear of failure hadn't stopped me before, back when I made them pay attention to me in auditions because I was good and brash and full of confidence. Where had that old spirit gone? I asked myself. In that moment the answer came back to me loud and clear: Nowhere!

I was still the actor I thought I was in *The Cross and the Switchblade* and *The New Centurions* and those early exhilarating days on

CHiPs. So what if the script was in Spanish? If Spanish was what it took to land the job, then I'd learn Spanish. After all, I had two whole months before shooting began.

The next morning I enrolled in the most intensive Spanish language course Berlitz had to offer, and for the next eight weeks I lived, breathed, ate, and slept in Spanish. Nanette even enrolled with me as a way to encourage me and help my progress. At the end of that time, not only could I speak Spanish fluently, I could read it like a native.

Which, deep down inside, was what I was. Taking those Spanish lessons and preparing to present myself to a Latin audience was the first direct link I'd had with my Puerto Rican heritage since Los Muchachos de San Juan, back in New York. It felt good, as if I were making another vital connection to who I really was. I had never paid all that much attention to that part of me before. I was rediscovering the blood tie I had with a whole world of brown-skinned people, whose values and way of life, whose emphasis on family and personal loyalty and hard work, had been so important in shaping me. Taking that job, and taking on the responsibility of doing it right, brought me face-to-face with the reality of my Latin identity. It was something I would learn to hold on to as a precious gift from then on.

Chapter Eighteen

The original run of *Dos Mujeres, Un Camino* was supposed to be the one hundred episodes that are standard for a Mexican telenovela. My contract called for four months of location work in Mexico City before I could go home.

But it didn't work out that way. From almost the first day the program aired, it was obvious we had a major hit on our hands. Letters to my character, Johnny, poured in from across Mexico, more than in those prime seasons of *CHiPs*, and soon they were followed by fan mail from throughout Central and South America. What originally had been scheduled to be a hundred episodes stretched into more than four hundred shows, the longest-running, and highest-rated, telenovela in Latin American history. And what had once been considered a program strictly for Spanish-speaking audiences was dubbed back into English when the series was bought by Rupert Murdoch for his worldwide broadcasting company, The Star Channel. Now called *Two Women, One Direction*, the show became a hit in such far-flung locales as Turkey, Hungary, Italy, France, and the United Kingdom.

From an American television actor, I had suddenly become a star of international proportions. Everything that had happened to me with *CHiPs*, the media attention, the screaming fans, the film and television offers, was repeated South of the Border, but with one significant difference. Respect. The newspapers treated me with esteem, and if anyone knew about those ugly rumors that had followed me for so long in America, they never brought them up. I was back on top, in a way that I could hardly have imagined even a few months before.

I had a great, lush Mexico City penthouse suite, along with a cook, a chauffeur, and everything else I'd come to take for granted during my heyday. And I was grateful to all the fans who took me and my character to heart.

When I started the show my Spanish was as good as anyone else's in the cast. Maybe it was even a little more proper and polished than that of some of the Mexican actors, but I made sure I was getting it right by studying the next day's script each night after shooting. I wanted to do the best job I could, and when I was named Best Actor in the Latin American equivalent of the Emmy Awards—the Hacé Awards—I knew that my efforts had been recognized.

But the truth was, I had already been a television star. I had waited so long for a shot to get back on top that it seemed a little strange to me when I got it, and it really wasn't all I'd imagined. To be working again was great, and to have some money in the bank was a nice change. But somewhere along the way, fame had lost its power over me. The second time around I knew what was important, and her name was Nanette.

I wasn't down in Mexico City more than a few weeks when I really started missing her. For all the wonderful accommodations Mr. La Rosa provided for me, probably the biggest single expense was paying my phone bill back to L.A. I was talking with Nanette every ten minutes, it seemed. When word came that my four-month contract was being extended, I really had to fight the resentment and remind myself that even though I would be away from my best friend for that much longer, I was being well paid and was well on the way toward the goal of rebuilding my career.

The long months of shooting *Dos Mujeres, Un Camino* were filled with exhausting days on the set and lonely nights in my penthouse, hitting my Spanish lessons. It was completely different from my early days in the business, when after a day under the bright lights of a soundstage I would head out for the bright lights of the nightlife. This time I just wanted to take care of myself, get plenty of rest, and get back home as soon as possible.

As a result, I have to admit that I didn't get to know my co-stars as well as I might have. When I wasn't on the set I usually could be found hanging out in the production office, talking to the secretaries and stagehands, trying to polish my Spanish. I've always felt more comfortable around regular people who reminded me of my own connection to the street.

After two months of working twelve- and fourteen-hour days, I couldn't stand it anymore. "Hey, Nana," I said during one of my endless calls. "Why don't you come on down here for the weekend? We can have a good time."

She agreed, but instead of a weekend, I held on to her for three solid weeks. When her work schedule got in the way, I convinced her to quit and come work for me, taking care of my house and business affairs back in L.A. I used any and every excuse I could find to lure her back to me. I even landed tickets to Michael Jackson's Mexico City concert and arranged for a meeting with the King of Pop himself, all for Nanette's benefit. And every time she got on that plane, I'd start thinking of another scheme to bring her back.

Finally, when all that traveling back and forth was really beginning to wear her out, I approached Mr. La Rosa and asked that he provide me with first-class air tickets round-trip from Mexico City to Los Angeles every weekend, so that I could visit her and my kids when I wasn't shooting. He agreed immediately. I will always have great respect for Mr. La Rosa for the way he treated me.

It was on one of those weekend visits, while Nanette and I were relaxing in the Jacuzzi, that I finally said what my heart had been longing to say for a long time. I'd been so afraid of taking that step, of saying the words I'd heard so many times from people who didn't mean it, the words I had used myself because I knew they would get me what I wanted; words that had no meaning until I looked into her eyes that night and knew that was the moment when it all suddenly made sense.

"Nanette, I love you."

She smiled, that same calm, centered, loving smile that had caught my eye across that crowded gym.

"That's good, Erik," she replied. "Because I love you, too."

Once those words were out, it seemed so natural, so right that I wondered what had held me back for so long. But whatever combination of doubt, fear, and burned fingers had delayed that confession was gone now. For me, the next step was as clear as the sparkling lights of the Valley below us that night.

When I took that step, I wanted to make sure it was right. My first marriage had been a stupid, spur-of-the-moment elopement. The second happened under the gun of a pregnant woman. This time I was going to do it right.

Six months later I made a casual suggestion for celebrating Nanette's upcoming birthday. "Instead of buying you some trinket," I said, "let's go down the coast to a nice hotel for the weekend. You can bring along your mom and your aunt and I'll call a couple of old friends and we can have a quiet little gathering."

"Sounds good," she said.

The next day we found ourselves sitting on a balcony overlooking the ocean with a small party of friends and family, toasting Nanette with a bottle of champagne. Off in the distance I spotted a small dot in the sky, growing larger as it approached the shore.

"Hey, Nana," I said, "what's that out there?"

She looked up. "Probably just a plane," she said, and went back to talking to her mother.

The plane got nearer and I could make out the pilot in the cockpit.

"Nana," I said, "that plane's getting awfully close."

"It's okay," she said without turning.

"I think you'd better look at this," I insisted, carefully controlling my voice in the best acting job of my career.

"What is it?" she said, a little annoyed, and at that moment the plane took a wide turn, following the coastline and revealing a banner that it towed in its wake. NANA, the banner read. I LOVE YOU. WILL YOU MARRY ME?

Epilogue

L ike I said in the beginning, what you see is what you get. I wanted to write this book to get across one simple sentiment: I'm grateful for everything that's happened to me—the good and the bad, the right and the wrong, the pleasure and the pain. If there's one thing I've learned, it's that everything happens for a reason.

I'm grateful to everyone who ever took a chance on me, who loved me enough to let me learn life's lessons my way, who stood by me and picked me up when I fell. I'm grateful to my mother and sister and brother, Joey; to Papa Don Pino and Pete Panos and all the guys on Amsterdam Avenue; to my beloved padrino, Roger Fonseca; to Mervin Nelson and Rick Rosner and the people in Hollywood who taught me that you can be a success in this business and still keep your honor and integrity. You just have to try a little harder. And special thanks to Phil Suriano and David and Laura McKenzie and little Elizabeth for the love and affection they have given Nanette and me. And I'm grateful to my fans, the people, north and south of the Mexican border, who always made me feel like someone special. And most of all, I'm grateful to Nanette, who taught me that true love is worth waiting for.

What you see when you look at Erik Estrada really is what you get. My life is an open book. The last page has yet to be written.

Index